Name_____

Count And Color

Read the number.
Color that many acorns.

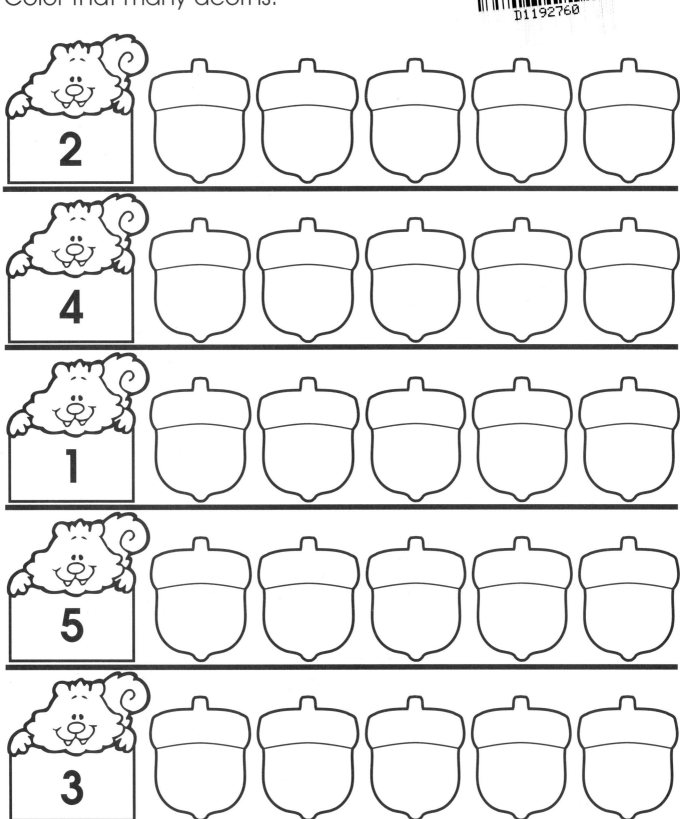

Name _____

Numbers And Nuts

Count.

 Color.  Cut.  Glue.

 **3**

 **1**

5

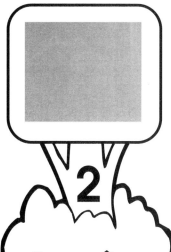 **2**

4

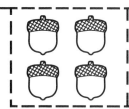

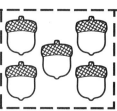

Name _____

Brown Bag Goodies

Read the number.
Draw that many nuts in each bag.

Name

is nuts about

counting!

Teacher

1 2 3 4 5 6 7 8 9 10

©The Education Center, Inc. • *The Best of* Teacher's Helper® *Math* • TEC3210

Name

is nuts about

counting!

Teacher

1 2 3 4 5 6 7 8 9 10

©The Education Center, Inc. • *The Best of* Teacher's Helper® *Math* • TEC3210

Holey Acorns

Count.  Cut. Glue.

| 8 | 5 | 7 | 10 | 6 | 9 |

Numeral Cards

Use with "Nutty Nibbler" on page 11.

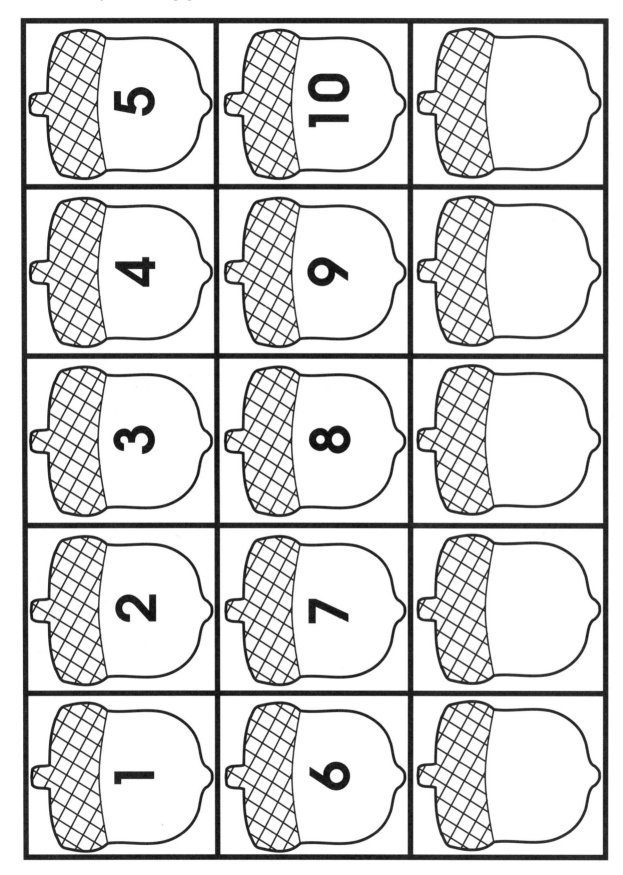

Nutty Nibbler

Color.

Cut.

Feed the squirrel.

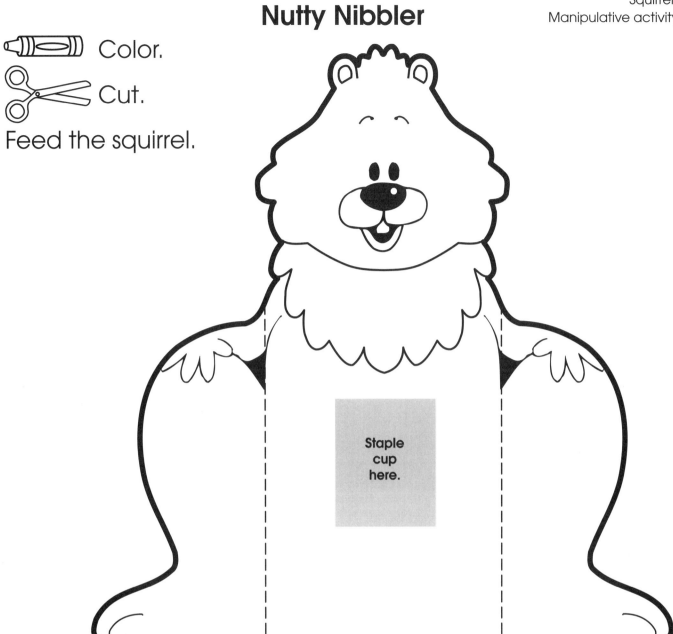

Staple cup here.

©The Education Center, Inc. • *The Best of* Teacher's Helper® *Math* • TEC3210

11

How To Use Pages 10 And 11

1. For each child, duplicate pages 10 and 11 on construction paper.
2. Have each child color the squirrel and acorns on page 11. Then assist each child in cutting out the squirrel, acorn cards, and acorn numeral cards (page 10). If desired, program the blank acorn cards with additional numerals. Help each child fold his squirrel pattern on the dotted lines, then staple a small paper cup where indicated.
3. To do this activity, a child chooses a numeral card, then places that many acorn cards in the cup.
4. For continued practice, send the activity home in a Ziploc bag with the parent note below.

Variation

If you have acorns in your schoolyard or access to any other types of nuts, use the real thing for this activity! Gather a supply of nuts and a large pail or plastic container. Enlarge and duplicate the squirrel and numeral card patterns on construction paper. Color the squirrel; then cut out the squirrel pattern and the cards. Tape the cutout around the pail or to appear as if he is peeking over the edge of the pail. In turn, have each child choose a numeral card, then count out that many nuts. From a designated place, have her try to toss each of the nuts, one by one, into the pail.

Use with "Nutty Nibbler" on page 11.

Dear Parent,

We have been feeding this little squirrel to help us practice numeral recognition and counting. You can help your child practice these skills at home with this nutty little activity.

To do this activity, have your child select a numeral card and count out that many acorn cards. (Use real nuts if you have them!) Have your child count as she "feeds" the nuts to the squirrel.

For a variation, have your child grab a handful of real nuts, then match a numeral card to the amount of nuts she has taken. By doing these activities, you are helping your child with some very important math skills.

So feed the squirrels!

Name _____

Designer Mittens

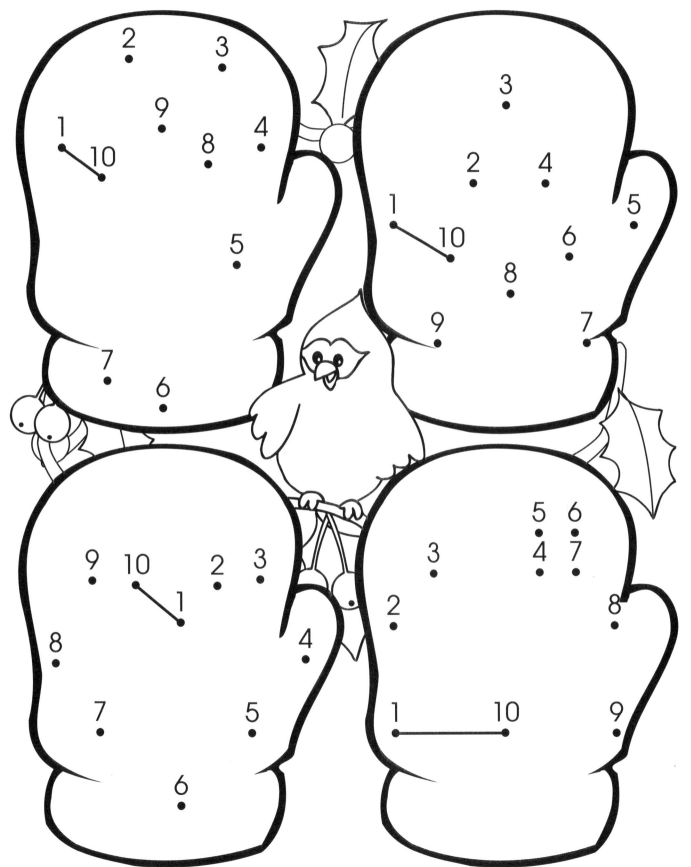 Connect the dots to make a design.

Extension Activies
Mittens

—Photocopy a large supply of the mitten cards below onto colorful construction paper. Laminate the cards; then cut them apart. Place all of the cards in a center and have each child use the mitten manipulatives as counters for working simple addition and/or subtraction problems.

—Photocopy several copies of the mitten cards below. Program each mitten with a numeral; then laminate and cut apart the cards. Store the cards in a decorated string-tie envelope. To use this center, a child sequences the cards in numerical order.

Finished Sample

Clothesline Count

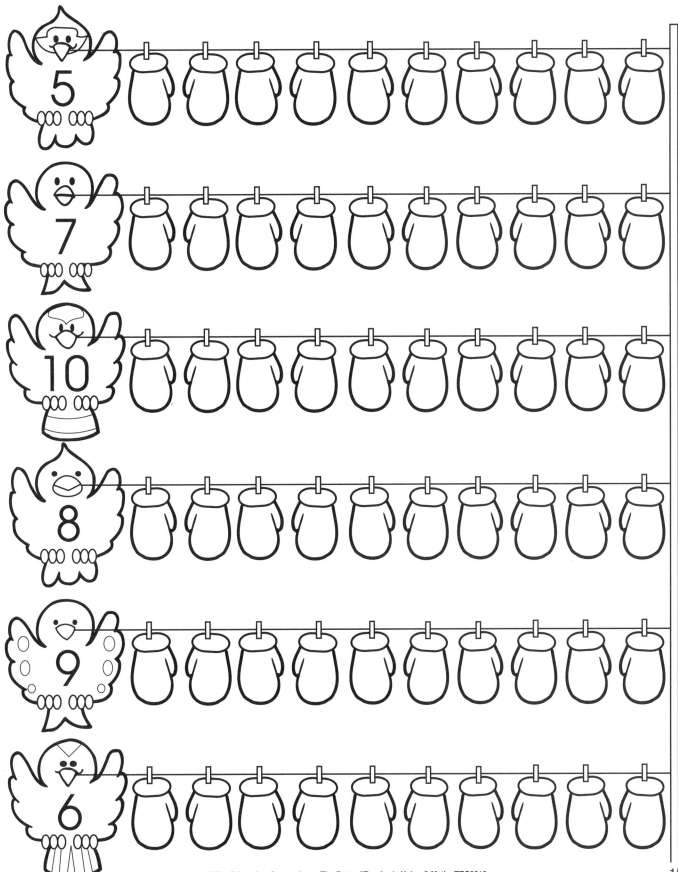

Color to show how many.

Name _____

Mitten Menu

 Draw bird treats to show how many.

Variations

— Supply each child with a plastic resealable bag containing some sunflower seeds. Have each child paste the corresponding number of seeds to each mitten.

— Use breakfast cereal instead of sunflower seeds.

Awards

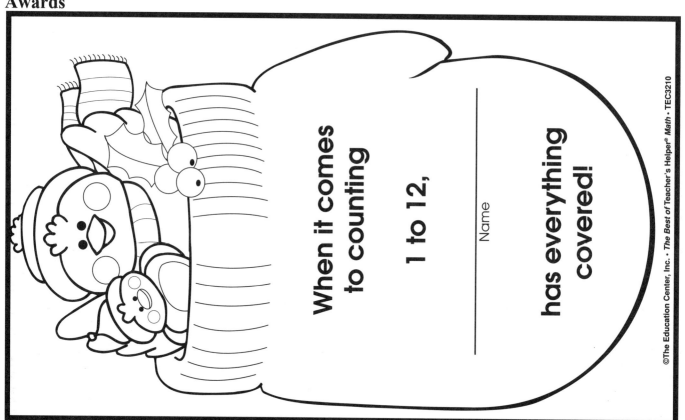

When it comes to counting

1 to 12,

_____
Name

has everything covered!

©The Education Center, Inc. • *The Best of Teacher's Helper® Math* • TEC3210

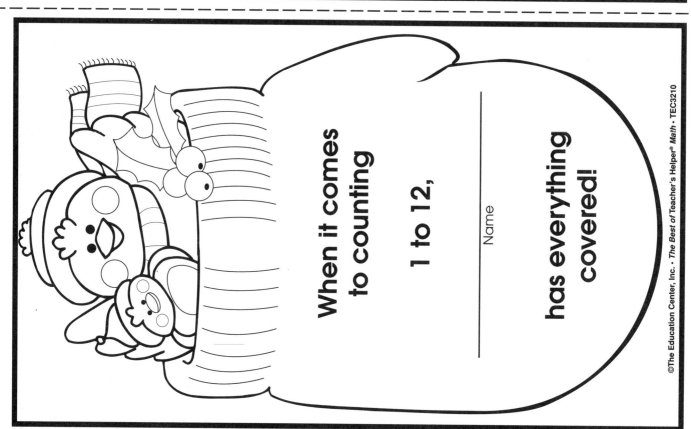

When it comes to counting

1 to 12,

_____
Name

has everything covered!

©The Education Center, Inc. • *The Best of Teacher's Helper® Math* • TEC3210

How Many Mittens?

Gameboard top

Gameboard bottom

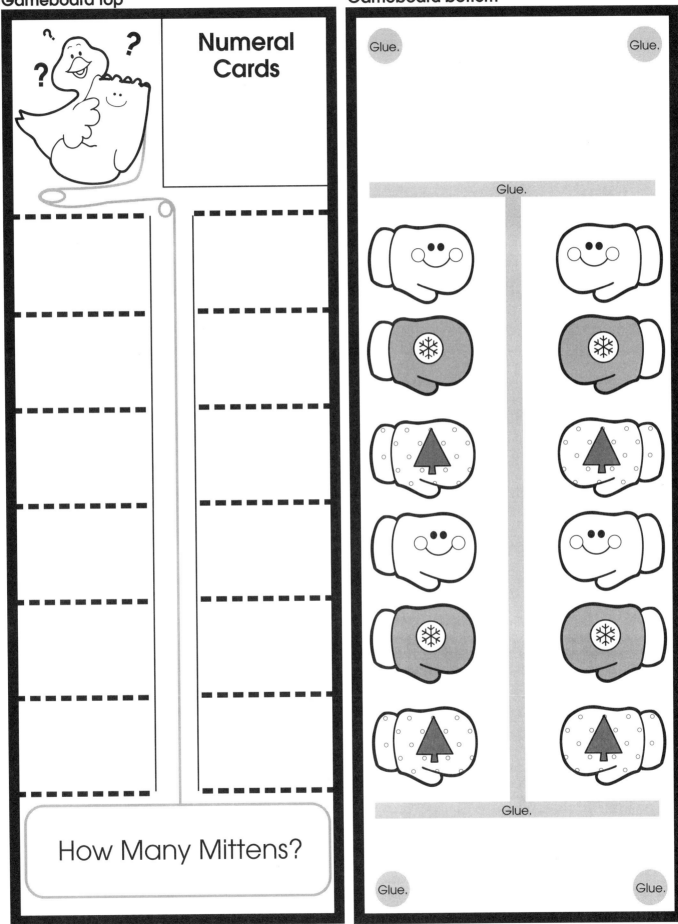

Numeral Cards

How Many Mittens?

Glue.

Glue.

Glue.

Glue.

Glue.

Glue.

How To Use Pages 19 And 20

1. For each child, reproduce both pages on construction paper. Have each child cut out the gameboard top and bottom on page 19. Then have him cut out the parent letter and numeral cards below.
2. Instruct each student to cut along the dotted lines on the gameboard top. Have him fold each rectangle on the solid lines to make "windows" on the gameboard.
3. Have each child glue the gameboard top on the gameboard bottom where indicated. Then have him glue the parent letter to the back of the gameboard.
4. To do this activity, follow the directions in the parent letter.
5. For continued practice, send the gameboard home with each child.

Finished Sample

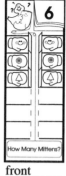

front   back

Dear Parents,
   We have been learning to count at school. You can join in the fun at home by playing this mitten counting game with your child. Begin by having your child identify the numbers stacked at the top of the game. Next turn the cards facedown; select the top card and open the doors over the mittens to show the corresponding number of mittens. Continue through all the numbers and repeat the ones that give your child the most difficulty.

Numeral Cards

1	2	3	4
5	6	7	8
9	10	11	12

Name _____

Snow Birds

Read the numeral.
Color the birds.

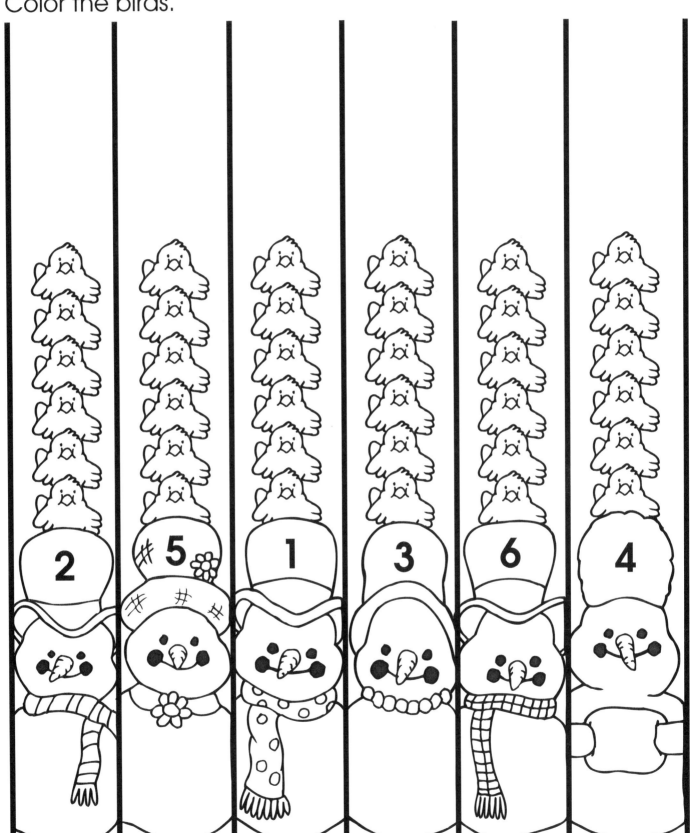

Frosty Friends

Read the numeral.
Draw buttons on the snowperson.

Home Sweet Home

Count. Cut. Glue.

| 7 | 8 | 9 | 10 | 11 | 12 |

25

Name _____

Follow Me!

Color.

Cut.

Glue.

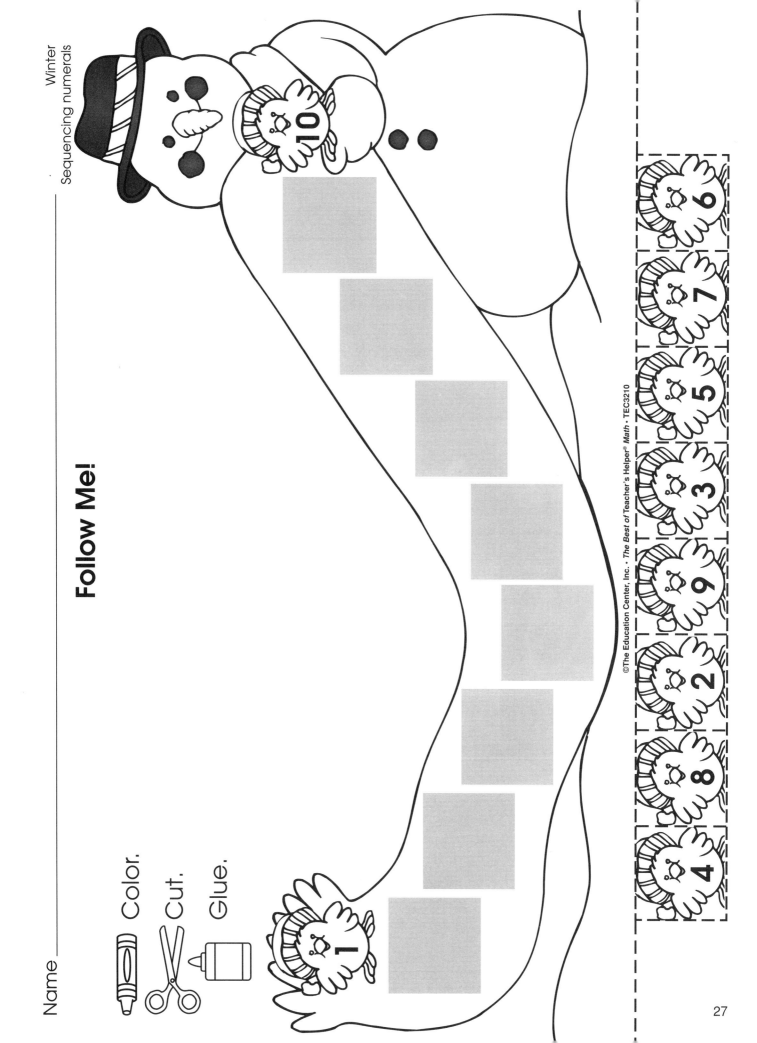

27

Name

is keeping it
COOL
with counting!

Name

is keeping it
COOL
with counting!

Note To The Teacher: Duplicate the award for each child. Personalize and distribute when appropriate, to reward each child's counting progress.

Name _____

Counting Cookies

Count. Write.

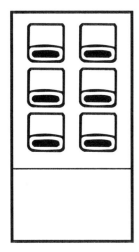

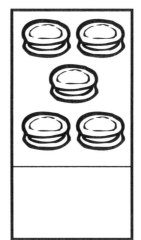

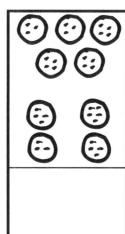

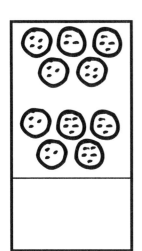

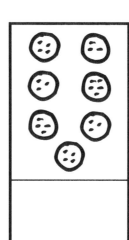

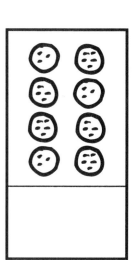

Draw **6 cookies.**

Extension Activities
Cookies

— Use felt cookies to play a subtraction game. Place several of these cookies on a flannelboard. Count them with your students. Ask your students to close their eyes. Remove one or more of the cookies; then ask students to open their eyes. With your youngsters, count the cookies on the flannelboard; then ask them to determine how many cookies are missing or how many are left.

— Provide each child with assorted cookies—such as wafers, fruit-filled cookies, gingerbread cookies, sandwich cookies, and biscuits—or supply him with cookie counters (see page 34). Have him use the cookies or counters to create a pattern.

— For this activity you will need a supply of numeral-shaped cookie cutters, raisins or chocolate chips, and refrigerated sugar-cookie dough. On a sheet of waxed paper, have each child use a numeral cookie cutter to cut that numeral from flattened cookie dough. Direct him to put the corresponding number of raisins or chocolate chips on his numeral cookie. Bake the cookies according to the package directions and enjoy!

— Stock a center with miniature cookies and large index cards each programmed with a different numeral. To use the center, a child chooses a card, looks at the numeral, and places the corresponding number of cookies near the card.

Sweet Sets

Count.  Cut. Glue.

15

  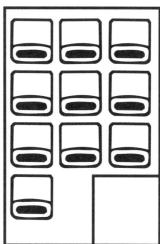 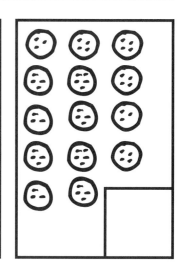

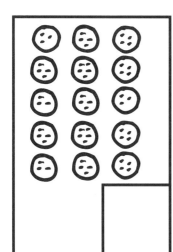 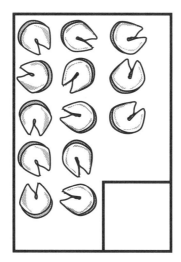 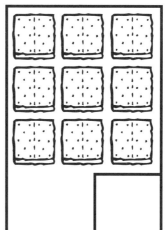

| 8 | 9 | 10 | 11 | 12 | 13 | 14 | 15 |

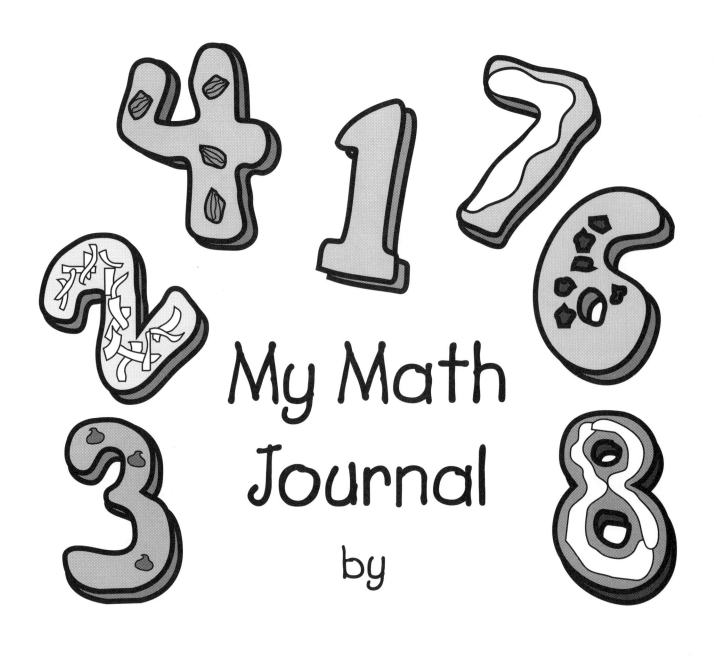

My Math Journal

by

Note To The Teacher: Duplicate this page on construction paper for each child. Have each child color her page, then personalize her journal cover. Place five to ten sheets of white paper the same size as this cover between the decorated cover and a construction-paper back cover; then staple the journal along the left edge. On selected days, have youngsters turn to a blank page and record the date; then assign them a math problem to solve.

Number Words
Minibook

 Color.

 Cut apart.

Put the pages in
order.

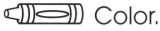 Staple.

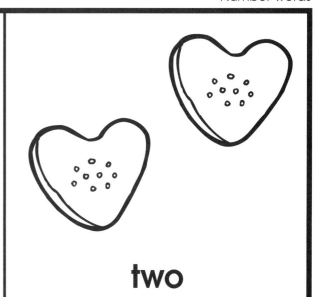

two

Counting Cookies

Staple here.

Cookies

©The Education Center, Inc.

three

one

four

©The Education Center, Inc. • *The Best of* Teacher's Helper® *Math* • TEC3210

Cookie Counters

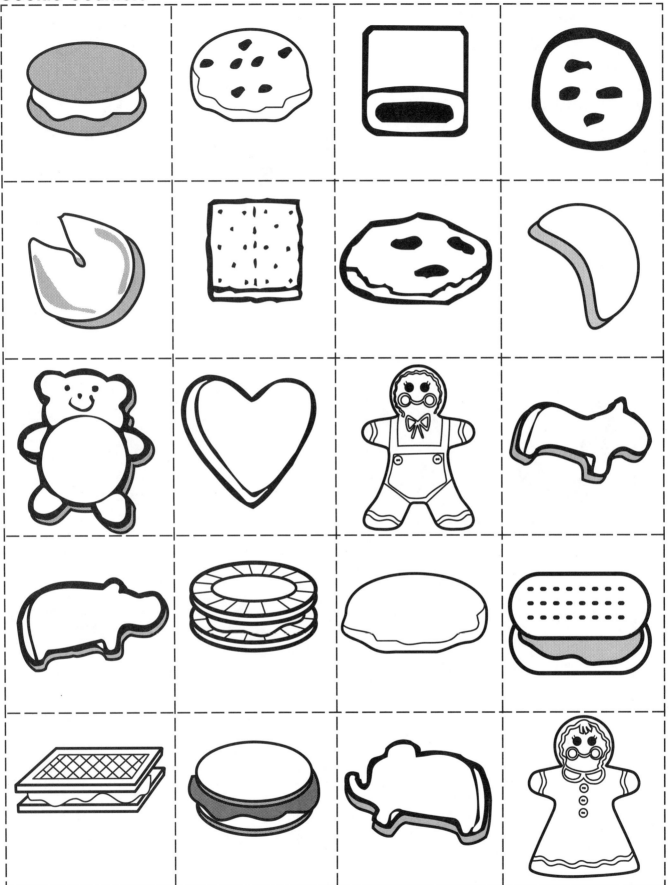

©The Education Center, Inc. • *The Best of* Teacher's Helper® *Math* • TEC3210

Note To The Teacher: Duplicate this sheet for each child. Have each child color the cookie counters, then cut them apart. Direct each child to use these counters whenever appropriate for counting, addition, or subtraction activities. Also use these with the second Extension Activity on page 30.

34

five

eight

six

nine

seven

ten

Note To The Teacher: Duplicate pages 33 and 35 for each student's minibook.

How To Use This Sheet

Reward each youngster for his good work by duplicating the award below and putting it into a resealable plastic bag along with a few cookies.

Award

did a sweet job on cookie math!

Name

©The Education Center, Inc. • *The Best of* Teacher's Helper® *Math* • TEC3210

Finished Sample

Snacktime Lineup

Listen.
Follow the directions.

cookie

How To Use Page 37

1. Duplicate the page for each child.
2. If desired, have youngsters write the numeral one under the first child on the page and the numeral two under the second child, then continue numbering the children through the fifth child. Review the ordinal number word for each child.
3. Have your youngsters listen to these directions and follow them:

- *Find the first child. Color the clothing on this child blue.*
- *Place your finger on the third child. Color this child's shoes brown.*
- *Locate the fifth child in line. Draw a hat on this child.*
- *Find the second child. Color this child's hair black.*
- *Place your finger on the fourth child. Color the clothing on this child green.*

Name _____

Kites In The Clouds

Read.
Draw bows on the kite tail.

7

1

5

3

6

2

4

Name

Polka-Dot Flyers

Count.

✂ Cut. 🧴 Glue.

| 5 | 9 | 10 | 7 | 8 | 6 |

41

Name

is a high flyer!

Great!

Terrific!

Wonderful!

Super!

Name

is flying high with good work.

Signed

Kites And Bows Counting Activity

 Color. Cut. Punch holes.

Finished Sample

String the kites and bows.

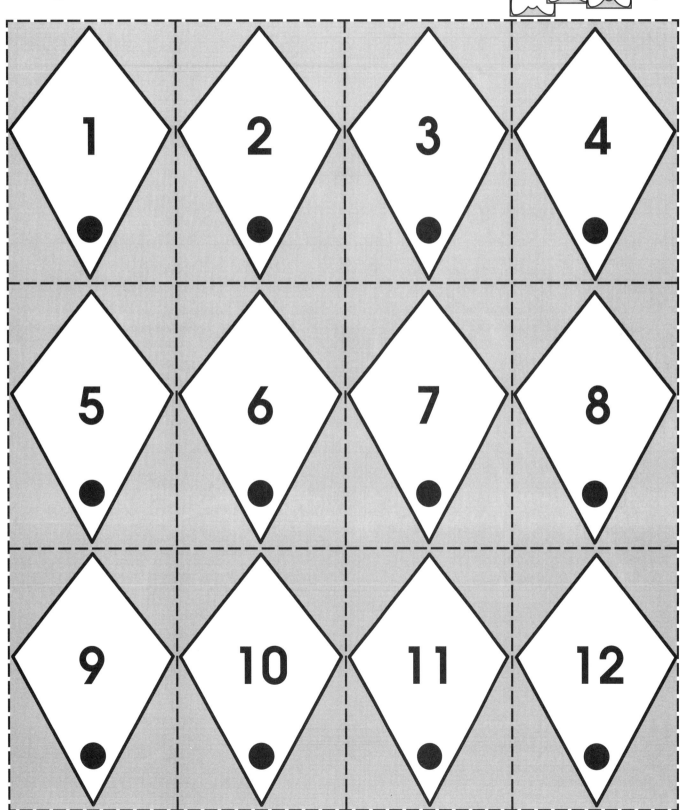

How To Use Pages 43 And 44

1. Duplicate one copy of page 43 and four copies of page 44 for each child on construction paper. (Duplicate several copies of the bow patterns below if more manipulatives are desired.)
2. Have each child color all of the kites and bows. Laminate and cut out the pieces; then punch a hole where indicated on each of the kite and bow cutouts.
3. Tape one end of a length of yarn to the back of each kite.
4. To do this activity, a child strings onto the yarn the number of bows indicated on the kite; then he tapes the back of each bow to the yarn.
5. To display these, mount large, cotton-covered cloud cutouts on a bulletin board; then attach the completed kites and bows.

Kites And Bows Counting Activity Pieces

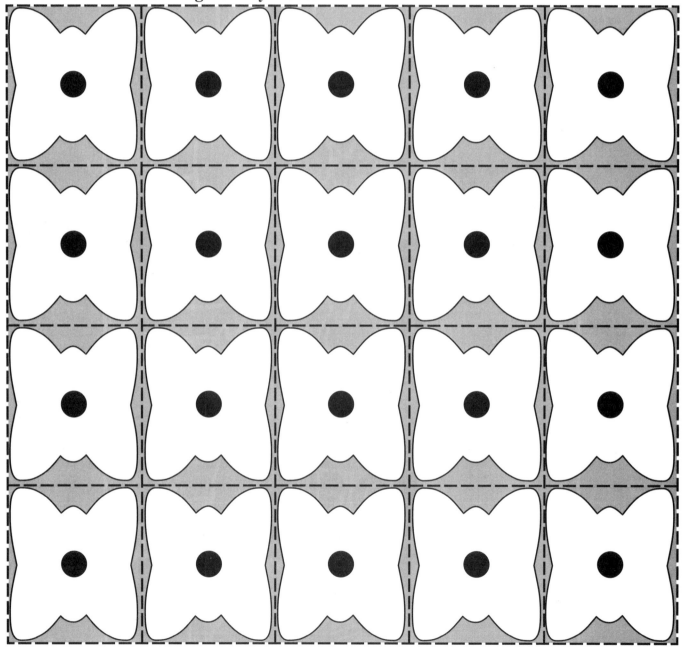

The Coconut Tree Counter

 Color. ✂ Cut. Glue. Attach.

Glue leaves here.	Glue trunk here.	Glue trunk here.
100	65	30
95	60	25
90	55	20
85	50	15
80	45	10
75	40	5
70	35	

Materials Needed For Each Student

— 1 construction-paper copy of page 45
— crayons
— scissors
— glue
— 1 brad fastener

How To Make The Coconut Counter

Help each student follow the directions below. Then have the child use her counter as a reference when completing the activities on pages 47, 49, and 51.

1. Color the page.
2. Cut out the tree trunk pieces, the leaves, and the monkey.
3. Glue the tree together as indicated.
4. Glue the leaves to the top of the tree.
5. Use a brad to attach the monkey to the top of the tree, as shown.
6. Practice counting to 100 by fives!

Variation

If this skill is not appropriate for your students, mask the numerals on a copy of page 45 and reprogram the tree trunk with a numeral sequence of your choice.

Finished Sample

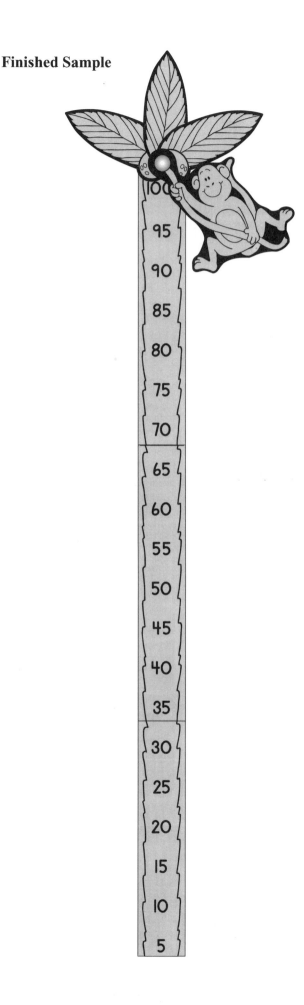

Name _____

Get In The Swing

✏️ Fill in the blanks.

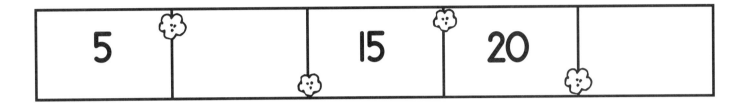

| | 10 | 15 | 20 | 25 |

| 5 | | 15 | 20 | |

| | 10 | | | 25 |

| 5 | | | |

🖍️ Circle the ten hidden **5**s.

Note To The Teacher

Duplicate this page several times on construction paper. Color the monkeys, laminate the pages, and then cut the cards apart. Use a permanent marker to program the leaves with a skill of your choice. (For example, program half of the cards with basic addition facts and the other half with corresponding sums.) Use the cards in a pocket chart with a group of students; or have individuals take turns matching the cards as a center activity.

Finished Samples

Programmable Activity Cards

The Wild Bunch

Count by 5s to 50:

| 5 | 10 | 15 | 20 | 25 | 30 | 35 | 40 | 45 | 50 |

Cut and glue to fill in the missing numbers.

| 5 | | | | 25 | |

| | | | 50 |

©The Education Center, Inc. • *The Best of* Teacher's Helper® *Math* • TEC3210

| 20 | 30 | 15 | 40 | 35 | 45 | 10 |

49

Note To The Teacher: Duplicate an award for each child. Personalize and distribute the awards to recognize students' progress in math.

Name _____

The Banana Stash

Count by 5s.

🖍 Color the boxes to show the way to the bananas.

Start

⭐5	10	15	20	25	12
	13			30	
48	64	45	40	35	86
24		50			99
18		55	60	65	70
37	61	39			75

How To Use Page 51

1. Duplicate the page for each child.
2. Have the class count to 100 by fives several times, using their coconut counters (page 45) as guides.
3. Instruct each child to color the boxes on page 51 as he counts by fives—from 5 to 75—to complete the maze and find the bananas. Encourage him to refer to his counter for help if needed.
4. Reward effort with some type of banana treat.

Variation

If this activity is too difficult for your students to complete individually, make an overhead transparency of the page and complete it together in a whole-group setting.

Name _____

Pumpkin-Patch Picks

Color the little pumpkins green.

Color the medium-sized pumpkins orange.

Draw faces on the large pumpkins.

Name _____

A Spooky Set

🖍 Color the set.

🖍 Color the thing that belongs in the set.

Staple bag here.

No tricks,
just a treat!
Watch my "spook-tacular"
sorting feat!
(Then help me eat!)

©The Education Center, Inc. • *The Best of* Teacher's Helper® *Math* • TEC3210

Staple bag here.

No tricks,
just a treat!
Watch my "spook-tacular"
sorting feat!
(Then help me eat!)

©The Education Center, Inc. • *The Best of* Teacher's Helper® *Math* • TEC3210

Note To The Teacher: Duplicate an award on construction paper for each child; then cut the awards out. Staple a snack-size packet of M&M's® or Skittles® candies to each award where indicated. Give each child a reward after he demonstrates success with sorting skills. Encourage him to show off his new abilities to his family.

Jack-O'-Lantern Sort

 Color.  Cut. Sort.

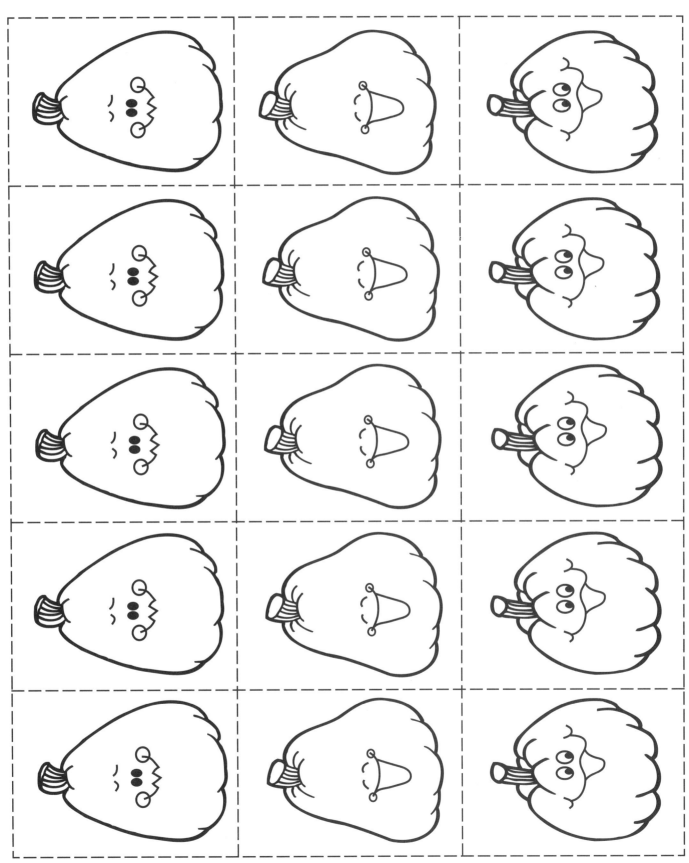

How To Use Page 57

1. Duplicate the page on white construction paper for each child.

2. Have each child color the pumpkins and cut them apart.

3. Direct each student to sort his pumpkins into three groups according to their facial expressions.

4. Give each child an envelope in which to store his pumpkin cards. Encourage him to take the cards home and show his parents his super sorting skills!

Extension Activities

— Have students make patterns with their pumpkin cards.

— Call out a number and ask each student to make a set of pumpkins to match the number.

— Use the pumpkin cards as counters/manipulatives to solve simple story problems. For example, "Three pumpkins are sitting in a patch. One is picked. How many are left?"

Hanukkah Fun

Graph. Count. ✏️ Write.

How many s? _____

How many s? _____

©The Education Center, Inc. • *The Best of* Teacher's Helper® *Math* • TEC3210

✂️ Cut.

🧴 Glue.

Note To The Teacher
Holiday Graphing

This graphing unit was designed using the same basic format so that after you explain the first page, students can complete the rest of the pages with little instruction. Happy holidays!

Background For The Teacher
Hanukkah

Hanukkah (also spelled *Hannuka* or *Chanukah*) is a Jewish celebration that falls during November or December. The story of Hanukkah began in 165 B.C. when a small Jewish army reclaimed their Temple from the Syrians after years of struggle. When searching through their Temple to find oil to light their holy lamp, they found only one small container of oil, which would light the lamp for just one day. This small container of oil, however, yielded enough oil to keep the lamp burning for eight days.

Hanukkah, which is also known as the *Feast Of Lights* or the *Feast Of Dedication,* is remembered each year by Jewish people with an eight-day celebration. On the first night of Hanukkah, a candle is lit on a candelabrum called a *menorah.* A menorah holds nine candles. The center candle, called a *shammash,* is used to light the other candles. On each of the remaining nights of Hanukkah, an additional candle is lit. During this celebration, Jewish families often exchange gifts, sing songs, and play games.

Name_____

Piñata Party

Count the piñatas.

Color the graph.

Background For The Teacher
Posada

Every evening from December 16 to December 24, Mexicans celebrate the biblical journey of Joseph and Mary and their search for shelter. This celebration is called *Posada,* which means "lodging." Participants sing and carry lighted candles as they walk to a predetermined house. Upon reaching their destination, half of the group goes inside while the other half remains outside singing a request for lodging. Several times the people inside the house refuse this request. Finally the door is opened, and everyone goes inside for additional festivities including feasting and the breaking of the piñata.

St. Lucia's Lights

Count the candles.
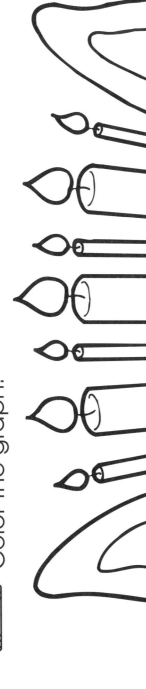 Color the graph.

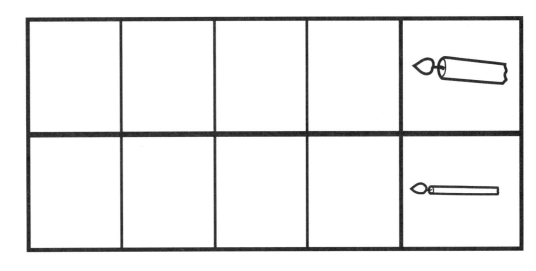

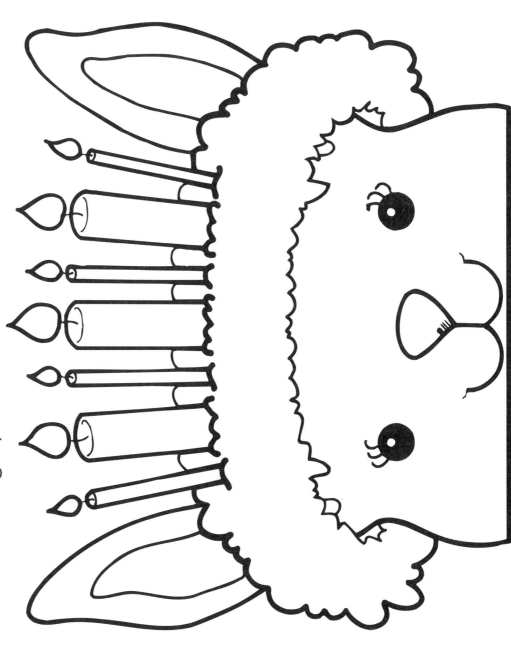

Background For The Teacher
St. Lucia's Day

On December 13, a day near the winter solstice—the shortest day of the year—a special breakfast is held in Sweden to honor St. Lucia. St. Lucia's name means "light"; therefore she has become a symbol of hope and the promise of spring at the darkest time of the year. The traditional custom in Sweden is for the eldest daughter of the family to dress in a long, white robe and wear a wreath of lighted candles on her head as she brings pastries and coffee to her family members on the morning of St. Lucia's Day.

Let's Decorate!

Count the ornaments.

🖍 Color the graph.

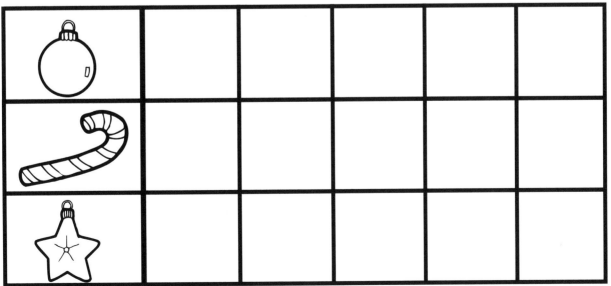

Background For The Teacher
Christmas Trees

In medieval Germany, an evergreen tree decorated with apples was used in the annual play about Adam and Eve that was held on December 24. This evergreen represented the "Paradise Tree." It is believed that the Christmas tree probably derived from the tree in this play because, by 1605, Germans began decorating evergreen trees in their homes for Christmas. Early decorations for these trees included fruits, nuts, lighted candles, and paper roses.

Christmas trees were first used in the United States in the early 1800s by German settlers in Pennsylvania. But it didn't take long for the Christmas tree–trimming custom to spread throughout the world. Today's decorations include tinsel, bright ornaments, electric lights, and candy canes. A star is often mounted on top of many Christmas trees to represent the star that led the wise men to Bethlehem, where Jesus was born.

Kwanzaa Candles

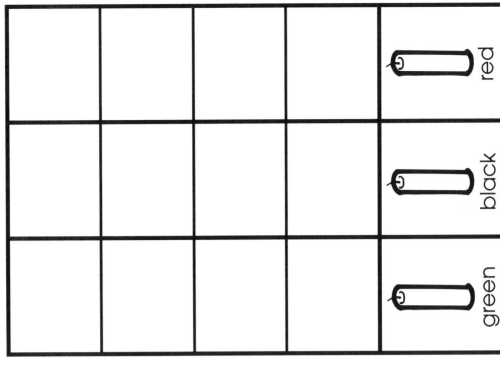

Count the Kwanzaa candles.
Color the graph.

		green	black	red

Color the candles.

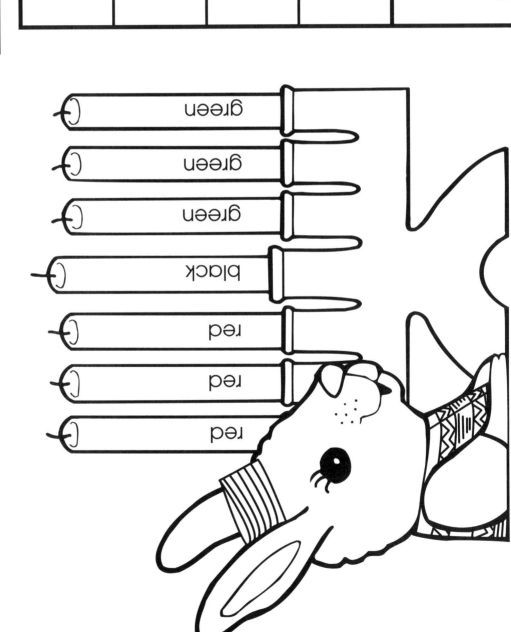

green green green black red red red

Background For The Teacher
Kwanzaa

Kwanzaa is a holiday celebrated by Black Americans. It lasts from December 26 through January 1. The word *kwanza* means "first" in the African language of Swahili. It stands for the first fruits at harvesttime. The *a* was added at the end to give *Kwanzaa* seven letters to match its seven principles.

This holiday began in 1966 and was created by Dr. Maulana Karenga, an African-American leader and teacher. He felt as though Black Americans needed to build their unity and strength as families. He wanted his people to understand their history and culture and be proud of them.

The seven principles of Kwanzaa are as follows: *unity, self-determination, collective work and responsibility, cooperative economics, purpose, creativity,* and *faith.* Each of these principles is represented by a candle held in a candleholder called a *kinara.* The three red candles and three green candles are separated by a black candle in the middle of the kinara.

Name_____

Happy New Year!

Graph. Count.  Write.

How many s? _____

How many ◯s? _____

©The Education Center, Inc. • *The Best of* Teacher's Helper® *Math* • TEC3210

✂ Cut.

🗴 Glue.

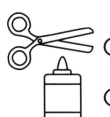
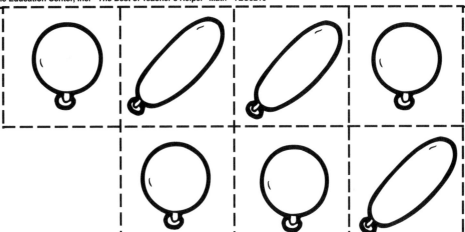

69

Background For The Teacher
New Year's Day

On January 1, people from all over the world who use the Gregorian calendar celebrate the arrival of the New Year. There are lots of parties and festivities held on the night before January 1—New Year's Eve. As the clock strikes midnight, people may sing, shout, make lots of noise, light firecrackers, kiss, or offer a toast to welcome in the New Year.

Some early customs for New Year include the following:
— the Romans giving gifts of gold-covered nuts or coins imprinted with pictures of Janus, the god of beginnings
— ancient Persians giving gifts of eggs symbolizing productiveness
— English husbands giving their wives money on New Year's Day to buy pins, hence coining the term *pin money*

Award

Happy Holidays!

_____
Name

is a
"gifted"
grapher!

_____   _____
Date   Teacher

Name _____

Graphing Gifts

What kind of gift do people like best?

Ask the people in your family.

 Color a box on the graph for each person.

My Family's Favorite Gifts

Happy Holidays!

a book   clothes   food   a toy

Trim The Tree

Count the ornaments.

 Color the boxes to show how many.

Write.

How many ⭐ ? _____

How many 🔴 ? _____

How many 🍬 ? _____

Which has
the most? Circle.

Mitten Graph

Cut and ✂ glue to match mittens on the graph.

Write.

How many _____ ?

How many _____ ?

Circle.

Which has the most?

©The Education Center, Inc. • *The Best of* Teacher's Helper® *Math* • TEC3210

Heavenly Heartstrings

Color the row of hearts that is longer.

Note To The Teacher

The reproducibles in this unit (pages 77–87) should be used as follow-ups to *concrete* experiences with comparisons. Consider using them only after your students have had many opportunities to participate in hands-on activities exploring these concepts.

Name _____

Post-Office Partners

Color: ♡ — red ♡ — purple ♡ — pink

79

Name _____

Red Hearts And Ribbons

Count. ▭ Color the side with **more** red.

Name _____

A Little Load Of Love

Draw a red ♥ around the heavy thing.

Color the light thing.

Name _____

Sweets For The Sweet

✂ Cut and 🍾 glue to match the candy.

🖍 Color the picture.

YOU'RE SWEET

Extension Activities
Valentine's Day

— Provide an assortment of valentines for students to look at to discriminate similarities and differences.

— Provide a supply of 6" x 2" and 20" x 2" tagboard strips, conversation-heart candies, and white glue. Invite each student to create a pattern with the hearts and glue it to a strip to make a sweetly stylish bracelet or headband. Did anyone create the *same* pattern?

— Have students brainstorm a list of different ways to say or show "I love you." Encourage them to add to the list as Valentine's Day approaches! How long can the list become?

Name _____

Hearts And Flowers

Put an **X** on the object that is different.

Color the objects that are similar.

Cow Coins

Draw an X on each penny.

Circle each nickel.

Draw a ☐ around each dime.

Milk Money

 Cut.

Match.

Glue.

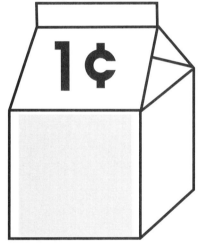 1¢

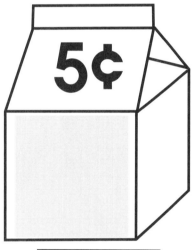 5¢

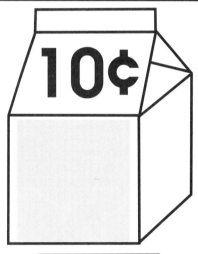 10¢

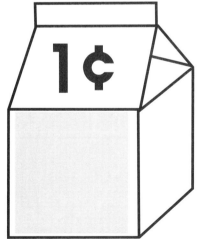 1¢

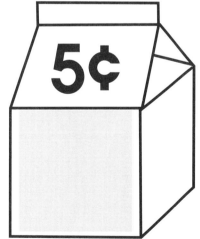 5¢

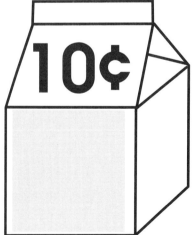 10¢

©The Education Center, Inc. • *The Best of* Teacher's Helper® *Math* • TEC3210

Making Big Money Manipulatives

Note To The Teacher: Duplicate the patterns several times. Color them using metallic crayons; then cut them out. Cut a round piece of tagboard the same size as each coin you will complete. Glue the corresponding front and back of each coin to opposite sides of that coin's round piece of tagboard. **Laminate** if desired. Place the coins in a math center for students to use as manipulatives.

Name _____

Spotty Cows

 Draw spots to show the value of each coin.

"Cow—abunga!"

_____

Name

is a crafty cowhand

at recognizing coins.

©The Education Center, Inc. • *The Best of* Teacher's Helper® *Math* • TEC3210

"Cow—abunga!"

_____

Name

is a crafty cowhand

at recognizing coins.

©The Education Center, Inc. • *The Best of* Teacher's Helper® *Math* • TEC3210

Barn Game

 Color.

Cut.

Assemble the brads.

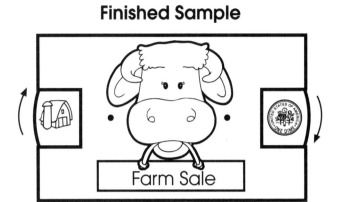

Finished Sample

Farm Sale

Turn the wheels.
Match a picture to a coin.

Farm Sale

Materials Needed
— crayons
— scissors
— tape
— sharpened pencil
— two brads per student

How To Use Pages 95 And 96

1. Duplicate pages 95 and 96 on white construction paper for each student.
2. Have students color page 95. Then have them cut out the artwork on page 95 and the wheels on page 96.
3. To improve the durability of this project, help each student attach a piece of tape to the back of each of his wheels opposite the dot and also to the back of his cow pattern opposite each dot.
4. Using a sharpened pencil, assist each student as he pokes a hole at each of the four dots.
5. Have each student use two brads to attach the wheels behind the cow.
6. To use the wheels for coin recognition practice, have each student repeatedly turn the wheels to match each coin with the corresponding picture.

Wheels

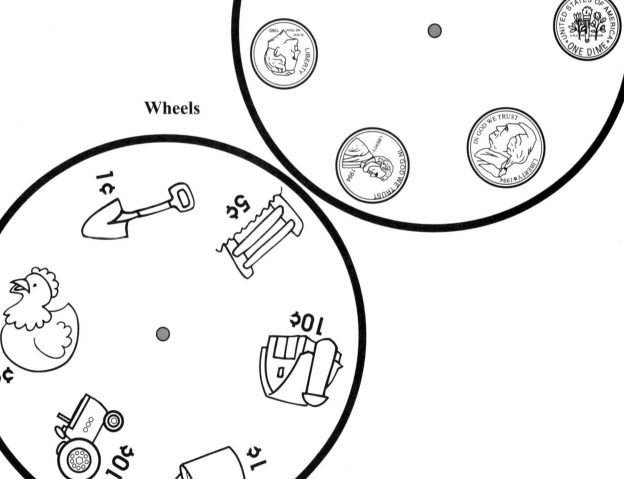

All About Pumpkin Seeds

 **Our pumpkin is:**

little

medium-size

big

Here is our pumpkin.

 I guess our pumpkin has  .

 I counted. Our pumpkin has .

 Here are my seeds.

Materials Needed

— miniature pumpkins (one for each small group of students)
— crayons
— knife
— art paper
— glue

How To Use Page 97

1. In advance, collect miniature pumpkins (roughly baseball size) for this reporting activity.
2. Duplicate the page for each child.
3. Divide students into small groups and assign each group a pumpkin.
4. To complete the page, have each student draw and color his group's pumpkin in the space with the pumpkin sketch.
5. Beside his pumpkin picture, have each child indicate the size of his group's pumpkin by coloring.
6. Cut open each group's pumpkin; then assist students in separating the seeds from the pulp. Arrange the seeds on sheets of art paper. Have each student estimate how many seeds there are, then write his guess in the space provided.
7. Next count the seeds to determine the total number. Have each student write the number of seeds found in his group's pumpkin.
8. When the seeds have dried, have each youngster glue a few in the space provided.

Finished sample

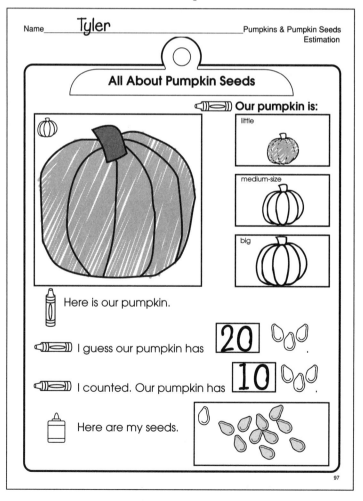

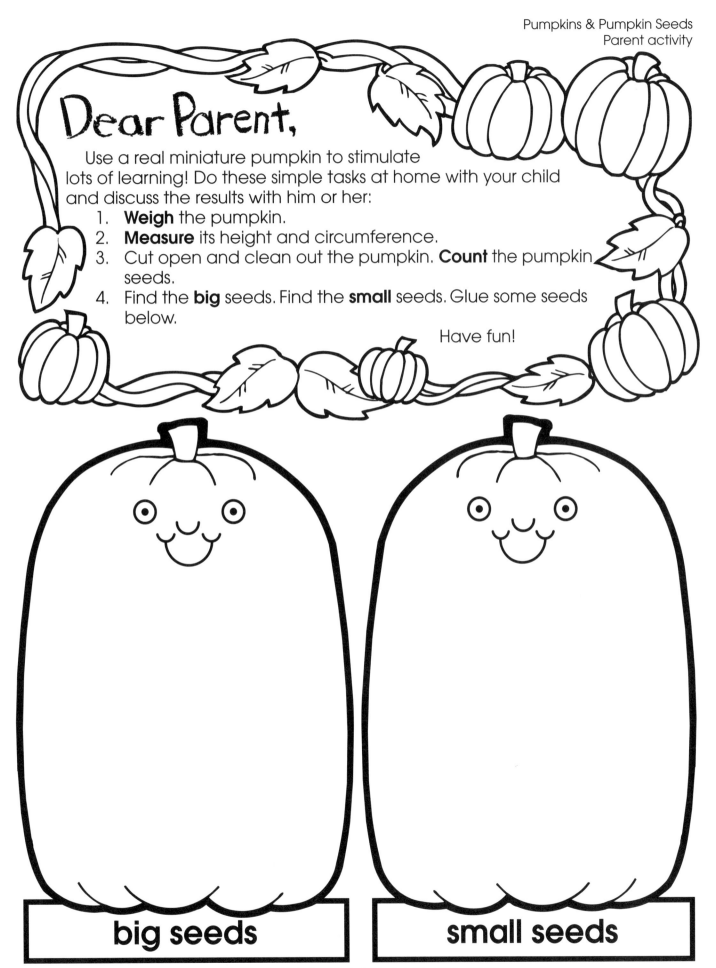

Dear Parent,

Use a real miniature pumpkin to stimulate lots of learning! Do these simple tasks at home with your child and discuss the results with him or her:

1. **Weigh** the pumpkin.
2. **Measure** its height and circumference.
3. Cut open and clean out the pumpkin. **Count** the pumpkin seeds.
4. Find the **big** seeds. Find the **small** seeds. Glue some seeds below.

Have fun!

big seeds

small seeds

Note To The Teacher: Send this sheet home for continued math practice.

Extension Activities
Estimating

— Cut open a pumpkin and let the children look inside at the many seeds. Ask each child to estimate the number of seeds he sees. Record each response on chart paper or on a large pumpkin cutout. Count the pumpkin seeds to see who had the closest estimate. Save the seeds for additional unit activities.

— Have each child hold a pumpkin and estimate its weight. Record each child's estimate on chart paper. Place each pumpkin on a bathroom scale to find out its exact weight. Compare the exact weight with each estimate. Discuss how many estimates were less than the actual weight of the pumpkin and how many were more.

Pumpkin Patch Counting

Count. ✏️ Write.

Draw. 🖍️ Color.

7
pumpkins

Playing With Pumpkin Seeds

Read.

Count.

 Glue or draw .

Name _____

Pumpkin Patterning

Glue on pumpkins.

Glue on pumpkin seeds.

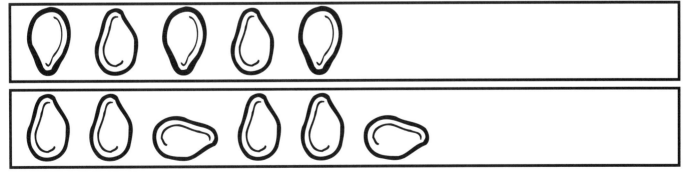

Pumpkins In A Row

Pumpkins come in different sizes.

 Cut.

Glue.

How To Use Page 107

1. Duplicate the page for each child.
2. Have each child cut out the pumpkins, then glue the pumpkins onto a strip of construction paper, in order from the smallest to the largest.
3. Have each child write the numeral one under the smallest pumpkin and the numeral two under the second-smallest pumpkin, then continue numbering the pumpkins through the fifth and largest one.

Finished Sample

Extension Activities

— Give students specific tasks to complete, using an ordinal number for each pumpkin. For example, have them color the first pumpkin orange, touch the fourth pumpkin, and draw a face on the third pumpkin. Continue in this manner until all of the pumpkins have been addressed.

— Provide youngsters with six different-sized pumpkins. Have your youngsters measure the pumpkins with string, yarn, or a measuring tape. Have students line up the pumpkins on a table, from largest to smallest or smallest to largest.

Name_____

The Bat Hotel

Trace.

Color the ⬜s blue.

Color the ⬜s yellow.

Shape Patterns

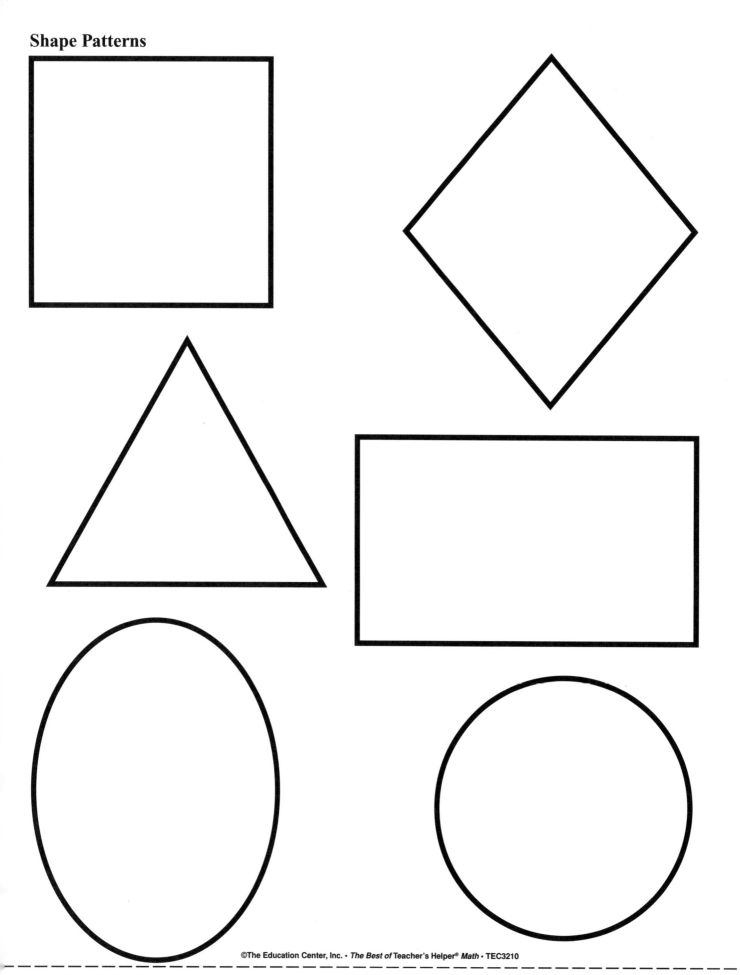

Note To The Teacher: Duplicate the patterns several times on construction paper; then cut them out.
110 Laminate them if desired. Place the shapes in a center for students to sort or pattern.

Bat Brigade

Trace. Cut.

Glue ○s on one wing and △s on the other.

111

Bats In The Belfry

Draw spiders on the bells.

Name_____

Baby Bats

Count.
Print the number.

Note To The Teacher

Duplicate this page several times on construction paper. Color the bats; then laminate them and cut them out. Use a permanent marker to program the bats with matching skills of your choice. (For example, program half of the bats with numerals and the other half with corresponding dots.) To do this activity, a child matches each bat to a corresponding card.

Finished Sample

Programmable Activity Cards

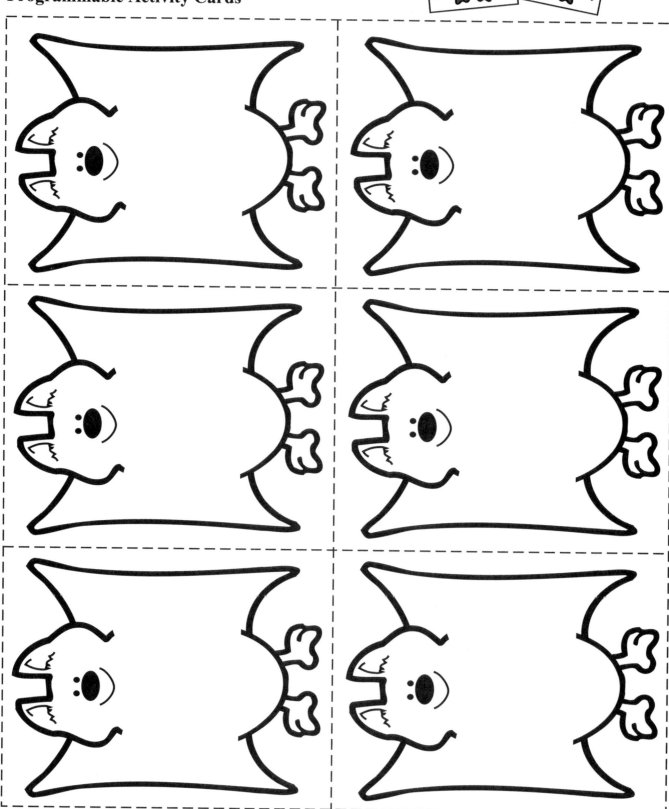

Name_____

Balls And Bats

Cut.

Match.

Glue.

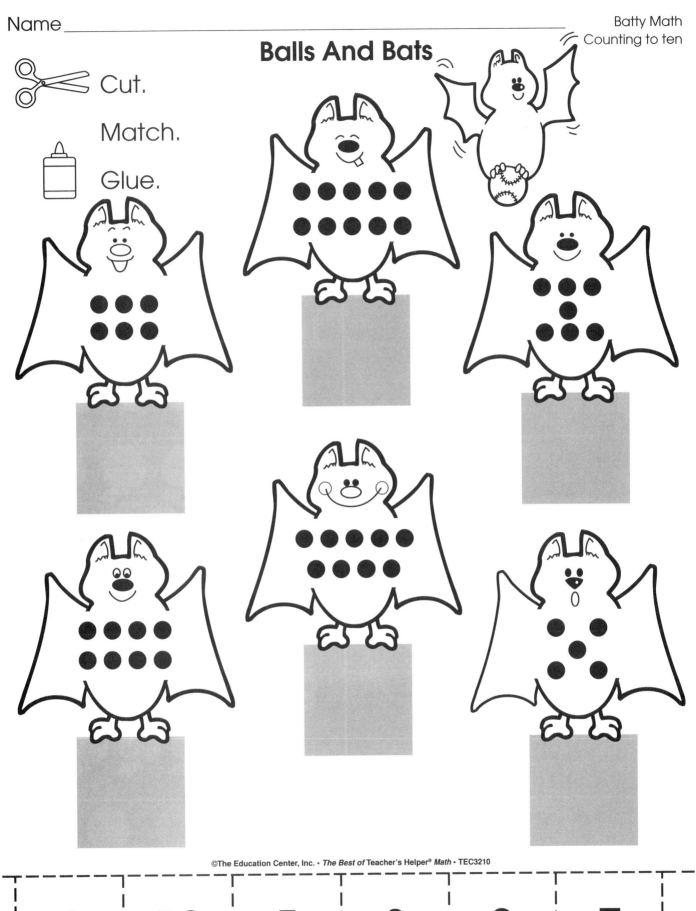

| 6 | 10 | 5 | 8 | 9 | 7 |

117

When it comes to
counting to 10,

_____

(student)

is a

High Flier!

When it comes to
counting to 10,

_____

(student)

is a

High Flier!

Batty Counting Gameboard

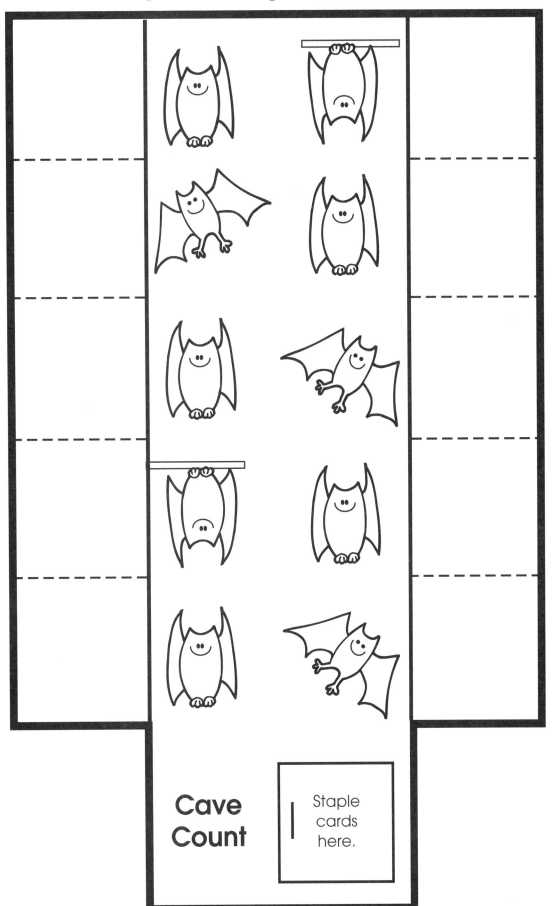

Cave Count

Staple cards here.

How To Use Pages 119 And 120

1. For each child, reproduce both pages on construction paper. Have each child cut out the gameboard and his numeral cards below.

2. Instruct each student to cut along the dotted lines on the gameboard. Then have each student fold the squares on the solid lines to cover the bats so they can hide in their caves.

3. Stack and staple the numeral cards (in random order) where indicated on the gameboard.

4. To play the game, have each child identify the numbers stapled at the bottom of the gameboard. Instruct him to select a numeral and open the caves to show the corresponding number of bats. Continue through all the numbers and have students repeat the ones that they had difficulty with.

Finished Sample

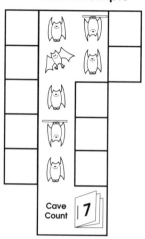

Numeral Cards

1	2	3	4	5
6	7	8	9	10

1	2	3	4	5
6	7	8	9	10

Dapper Apple

 Draw a line to match the words and numerals.

3

2

1

5

4

one

two

three

four

five

Bonus Box: Write numerals 1 to 5 on the back of this sheet. Draw apples for each numeral.

one	1 🍎
two	2 🍎🍎
three	3 🍎🍎🍎
four	4 🍎🍎🍎🍎
five	5 🍎🍎🍎🍎🍎

Note To The Teacher: Duplicate the cards; then cut them out. Laminate them if desired. Place the cards in a center. To use the center, a child matches a number word to a corresponding numeral card.

Name_____

Bananaberry Bunch

Read.

Cut.

Glue.

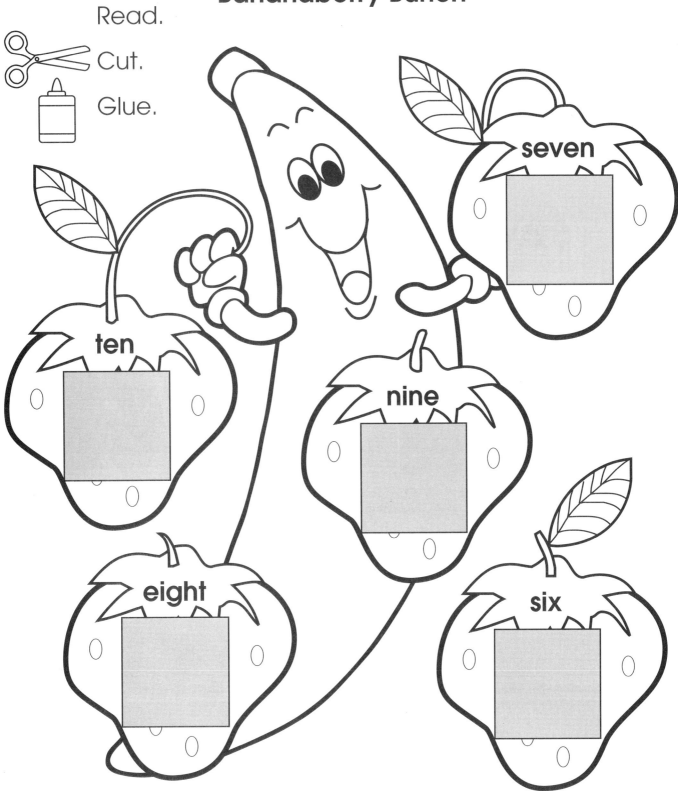

seven

ten

nine

eight

six

| 6 | 7 | 8 | 9 | 10 |

six	**6**
seven	**7**
eight	**8**
nine	**9**
ten	**10**

Note To The Teacher: Duplicate the cards; then cut them out. Laminate them if desired. Place the cards in a center. To use the center, a child matches a number word to a corresponding numeral card.

Fruit Salad Silliness

Color the set
that shows
more.

Rootin'-Tootin' Fruit

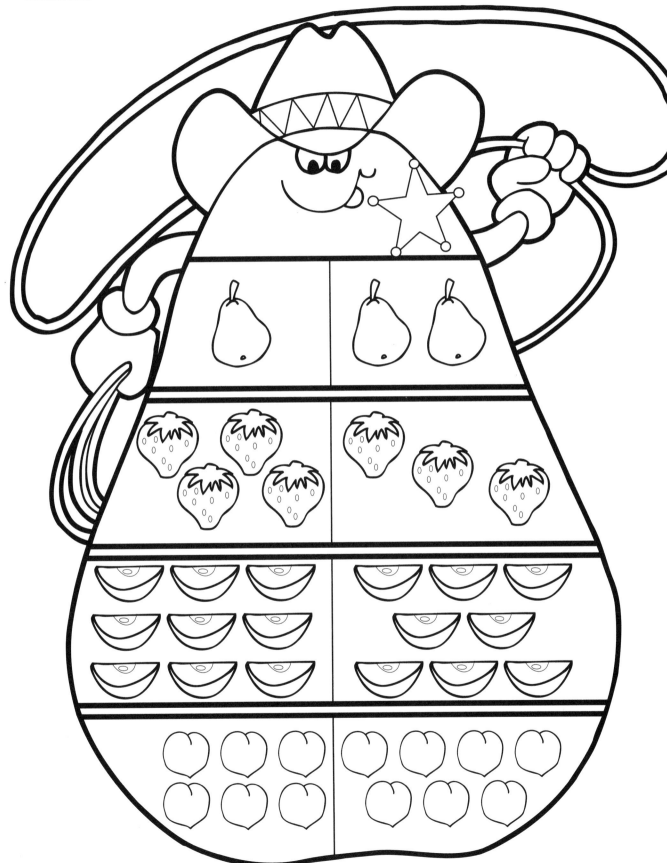 Color the set that shows less.

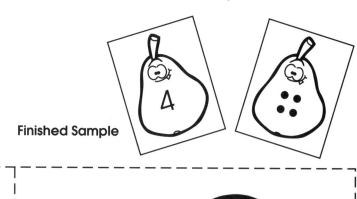

Programmable Activity Cards

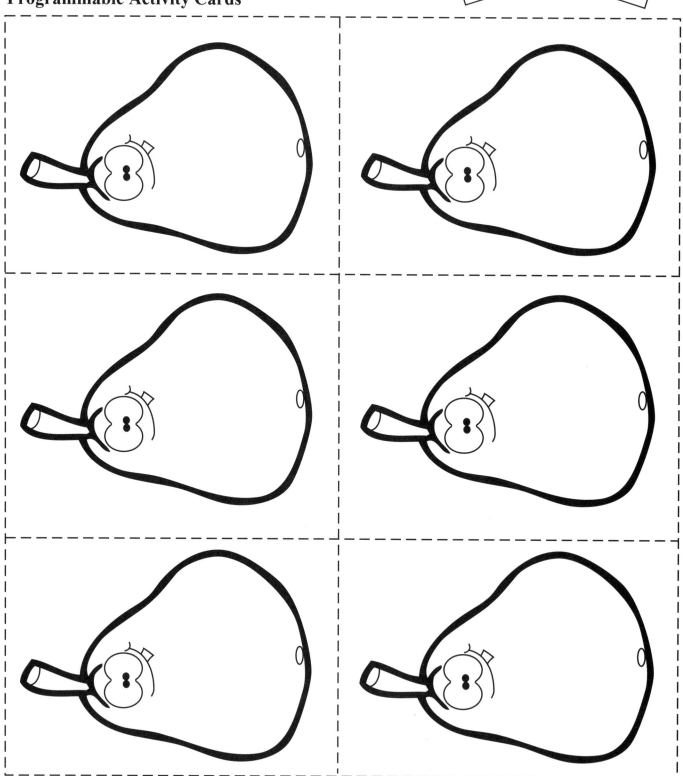

Note To The Teacher: Duplicate this page several times on colored construction paper. Then laminate the pages and cut out the cards. Use a permanent marker to program the fruit with the matching skills of your choice. (For example, program half of the fruit with a numeral and the other half with corresponding dots.) To do this activity, a child matches each fruit to its corresponding card.

Supersonic Strawberry

Begin at the ★.
Connect the dots.
 Color.

1 ★ Start

2

12

3

11

10

4

9

8

7

6

5

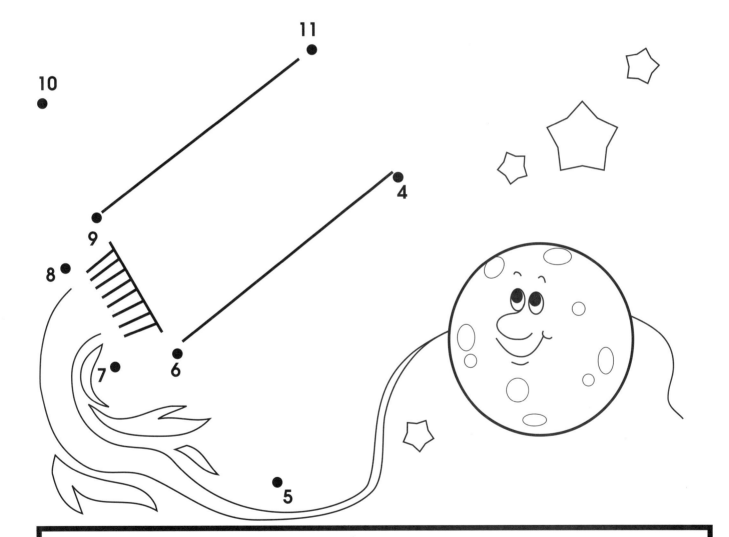

 Color 12.

Extension Activity

— In advance cut bite-size pieces of several kinds of fruit, such as apples, bananas, oranges, and grapes. Then blindfold each child in turn, and have him taste one fruit and try to guess the fruit. Continue in this manner until each child has had a turn. Then have each child draw, cut out, and graph his favorite fruit.

Award

Name _____

is

getting to the

core of

math skills!

Note To The Teacher: Duplicate an award for each child. Personalize and distribute these awards when appropriate.

Name _____

Corral Counting

Count.

Write the number.

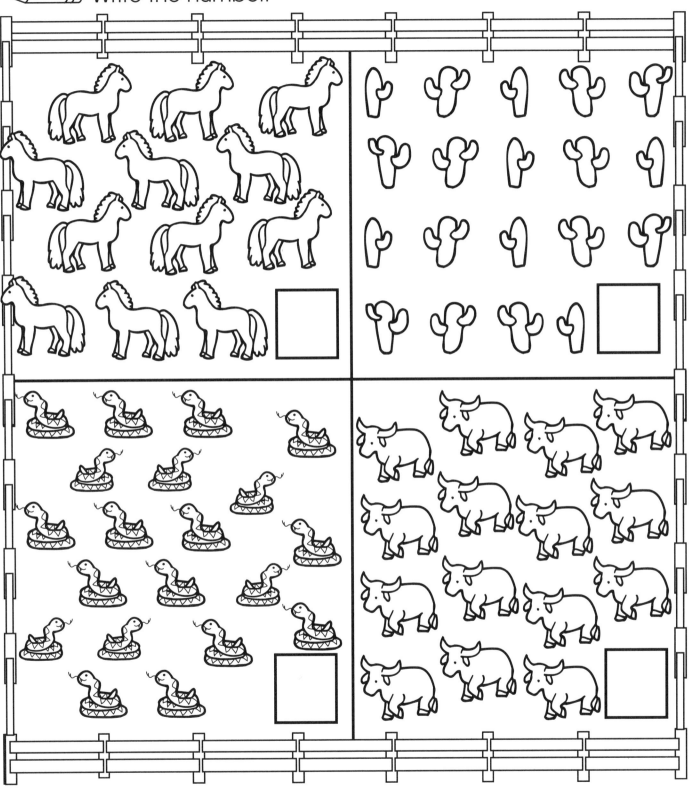

Name _____

Buckaroo Mouse

Add.

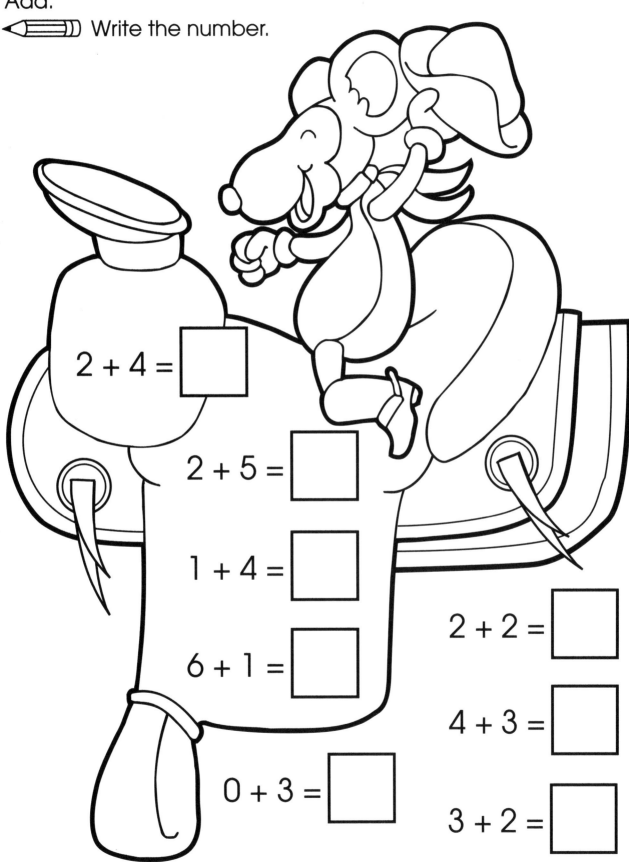
Write the number.

2 + 4 = ☐

2 + 5 = ☐

1 + 4 = ☐

6 + 1 = ☐

2 + 2 = ☐

4 + 3 = ☐

0 + 3 = ☐

3 + 2 = ☐

How To Use Pages 133, 134, And 135

1. Photocopy page 133, page 135, and the horse counters below for each child.
2. Have each child color the horse counters, then cut them apart.
3. Direct each child to use the horse counters to determine the sums, then write the correct numeral in the spaces provided.

Patterns
Horse Counters

Rootin'-Tootin' Boots

Add the numbers.
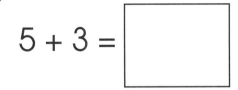 Write the sum in the box.

5 + 3 =

7 + 2 =

5 + 5 =

3 + 2 =

3 + 7 =

2 + 2 =

8 + 1 =

9 + 0 =

Note To The Teacher

Duplicate this page several times on construction paper. Color the cowboy boots, laminate them, and then cut them out. Use a permanent marker to program the boots with matching skills of your choice. (For example, program half of the boots with addition problems and the other half with the corresponding sums.) To do this activity, a child matches each boot to a corresponding card.

Finished Sample

Programmable Activity Cards

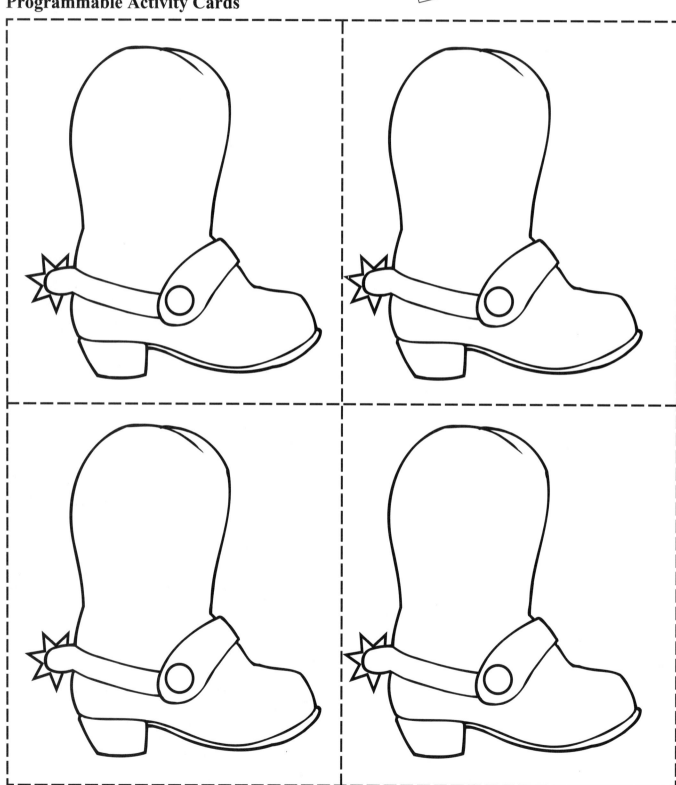

Fence By The Inch

Measure each fence.

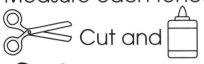 Cut and glue the number of inches.

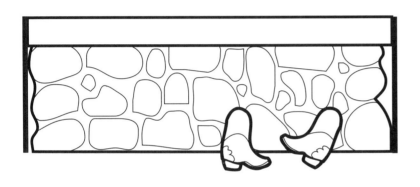

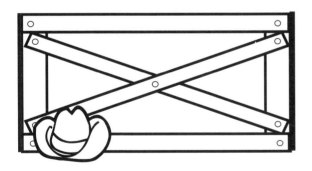

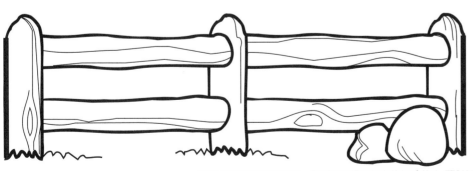

©The Education Center, Inc. • *The Best of* Teacher's Helper® *Math* • TEC3210

| 2 | 5 | 6 | 4 | 8 | 3 |

How To Use Pages 137 And 138

1. Duplicate page 137 for each child and duplicate several copies of page 138.
2. Cut the rulers apart on each copy of page 138.
3. Provide each child with a ruler cutout to measure each picture on page 137. Then have him glue the correct numeral in the space provided.

Rulers

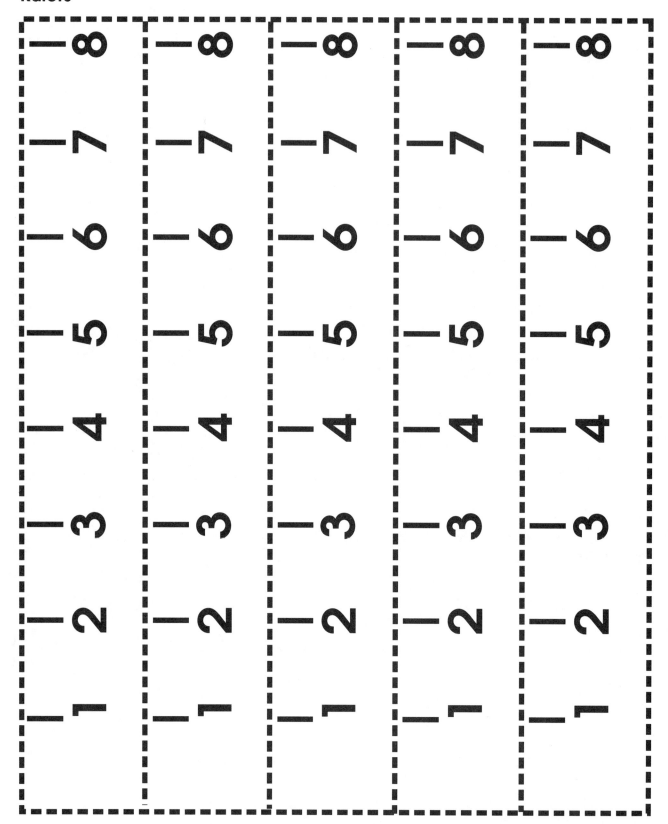

Cactus Cuties

How many inches?
Measure.

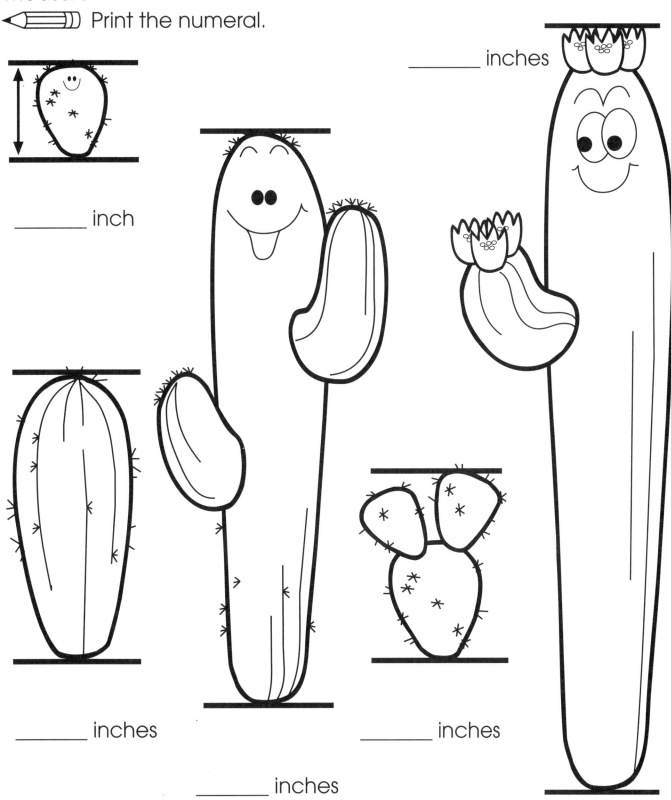 Print the numeral.

_____ inches

_____ inch

_____ inches

_____ inches

_____ inches

_____ inches

How To Use Page 139

1. Duplicate the page for each child.
2. Have each child use a ruler (see page 138) to measure each picture on the page, then write the correct number of inches on the line.

High Noon

 Write the time to match each clock.

____ : ____   ____ : ____   ____ : ____   ____ : ____

____ : ____   ____ : ____

____ : ____

Roundup Time

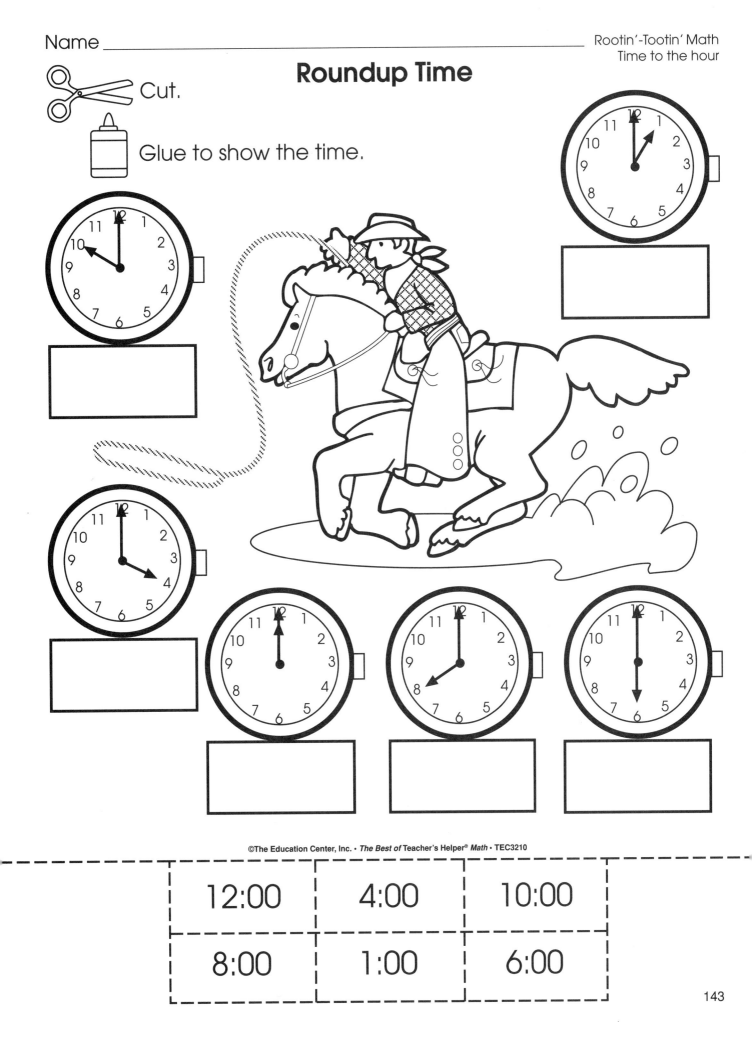

✂ Cut.

Glue to show the time.

12:00	4:00	10:00
8:00	1:00	6:00

143

_____

Name

is

really sharp

in math skills.

_____

Teacher

©The Education Center, Inc. • *The Best of* Teacher's Helper® *Math* • TEC3210

_____

Name

is

really sharp

in math skills.

_____

Teacher

©The Education Center, Inc. • *The Best of* Teacher's Helper® *Math* • TEC3210

Name

Frog Food

Count.

 Write how many are in each set.

Add.

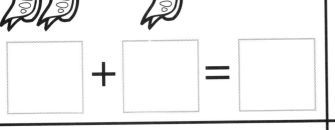

☐ + ☐ = ☐

☐ + ☐ = ☐

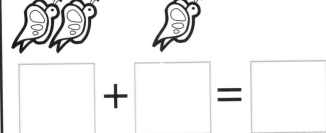

☐ + ☐ = ☐

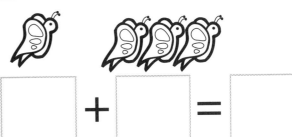

☐ + ☐ = ☐

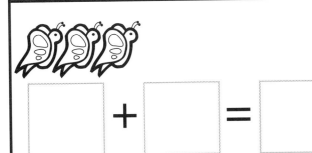

☐ + ☐ = ☐

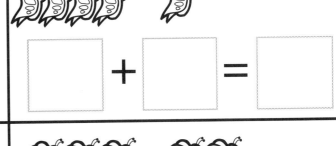

☐ + ☐ = ☐

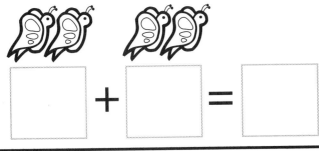

☐ + ☐ = ☐

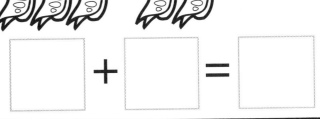

☐ + ☐ = ☐

Name _____

Spring Sunbather

Count.
Add.
 Write the number.

3 + 3 = _____	3 + 4 = _____
4 + 0 = _____	5 + 2 = _____
3 + 1 = _____	2 + 3 = _____
2 + 2 = _____	1 + 6 = _____

Note To The Teacher

Duplicate this page several times on colored construction paper. Then laminate the sheets and cut the frog cards out. Use a permanent marker to program the frogs with the matching skill of your choice (for example program half of the frogs with addition problems and the other half with the sums). To do this activity, a child matches each frog to a corresponding card.

Finished Samples

Programmable Activity Cards

Name _____

Leapin' Lily Pads

 Cut out the frogs.
Use as counters.
Add.

6 + 1 =

2 + 2 =   8 + 2 =

6 + 3 =   3 + 3 =

9 + 1 =   5 + 3 =

5 + 1 =   4 + 6 =

Name

is

hopping right along
with addition facts to 10!

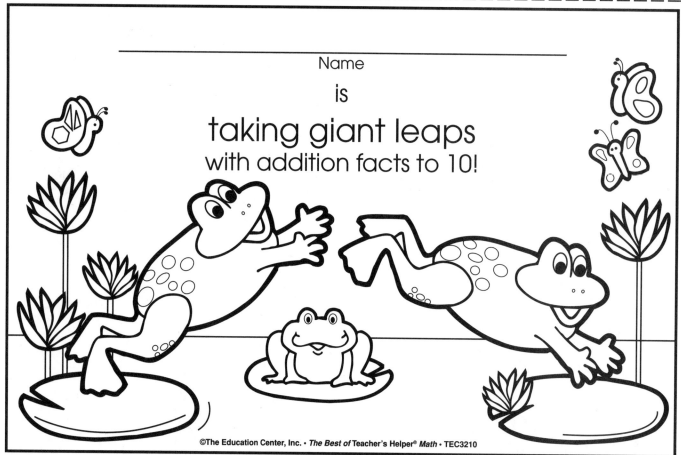

Name

is

taking giant leaps
with addition facts to 10!

Note To The Teacher: Duplicate an award for each child. Distribute the awards when appropriate to reward each child's addition facts.

Tick-Tock Tulip

Cut and glue the numbers on the clock.

Fill in the blank.

11

10

1

2

4

It is _____ o'clock.

7

6   9   3   12   8   5

151

Record Sheet

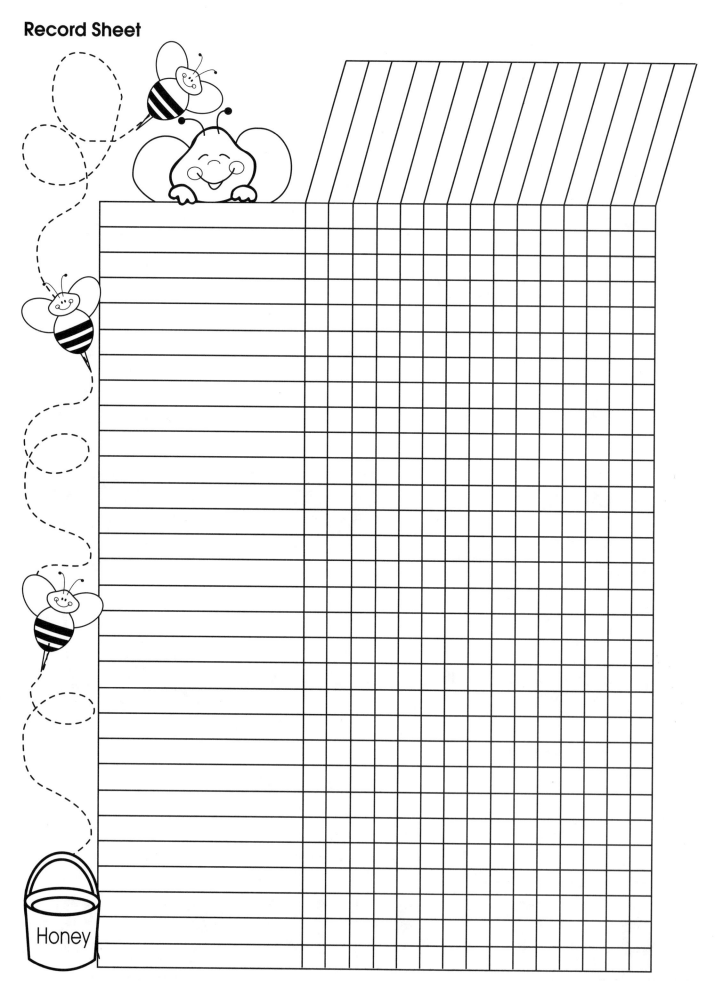

Honey

Sunflower Hours

Circle the box that shows the correct time.

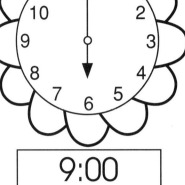

9:00
6:00

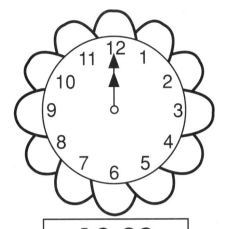

12:00
4:00

2:00
7:00

1:00
11:00

10:00
5:00

5:00
3:00

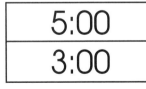

8:00
9:00

Honey

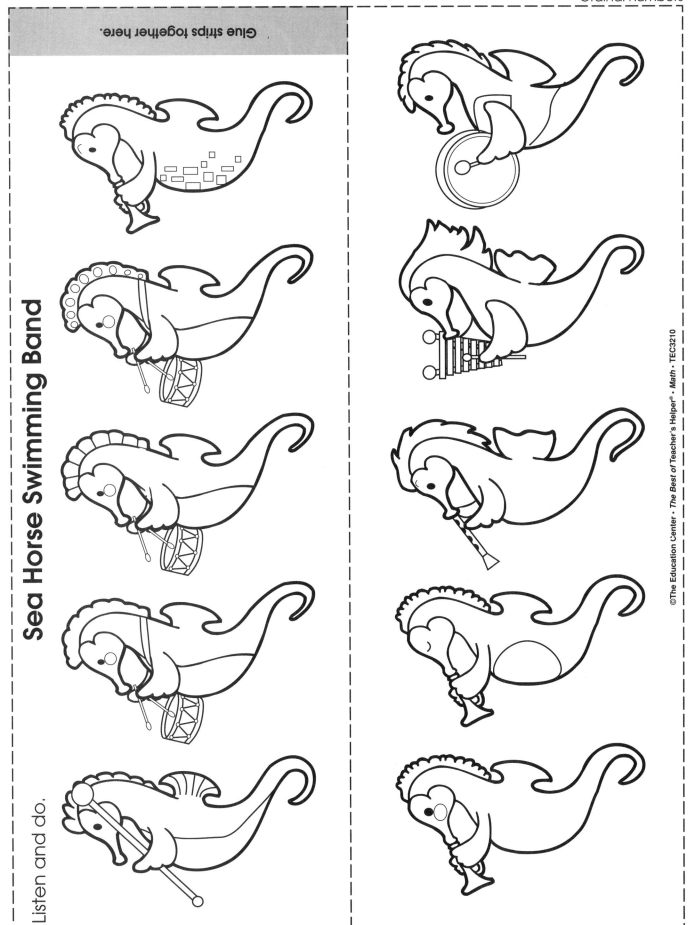

Sea Horse Swimming Band

Glue strips together here.

Listen and do.

How To Use Page 155

1. Duplicate the page for each child.
2. Have each child cut along the dotted lines, then glue where indicated on the gray area.
3. If desired, have youngsters write the numeral one under the first sea horse and the numeral two under the second sea horse, then continue numbering the sea horses through the tenth sea horse. Review the ordinal number for each horse.
4. Have your youngsters listen to these directions and follow them.

- *Find the second sea horse. Draw a blue hat on it.*
- *Find the fifth sea horse. Color it red.*
- *Locate the eighth sea horse on your strip. Draw purple spots on its stomach.*
- *Put your finger on the sixth sea horse. Draw a yellow circle around it.*
- *Find the tenth sea horse. Color its musical instrument green.*
- *Place your finger on the first sea horse. Draw brown sand under it.*
- *Count to the seventh sea horse. Draw blue bubbles next to it.*
- *Find the ninth sea horse. Color its tail black.*
- *Put your finger on the third sea horse. Draw a yellow crown on its head.*
- *Locate the fourth sea horse. Color it orange.*

**Finished
Sample**

Rhythm In The Waves

Add.
Cut.
Glue.

5   **6**   **7**

| 7 + 0 = | 3 + 2 = | 3 + 3 = | 4 + 3 = | 5 + 0 = |
| 1 + 4 = | 5 + 1 = | 4 + 2 = | 5 + 2 = | |

How To Use Pages 157 And 158

1. Duplicate page 157 and the sea critter counters below for each child.
2. Have each child color the sea critter counters, then cut them apart.
3. Direct each child to use the counters to determine the sums; then glue the correct number sentences in the shaded spaces provided.

Sea Critter Counters

Use with "Rhythm In The Waves" on page 157.

Symphonic Sea Horses

Add.
Write the answer.

3 + 4 =

3 + 6 =

4 + 4 =

0 + 9 =

1 + 6 =

6 + 2 =

2 + 5 =

4 + 5 =

_____
(student)

is right on key when it comes to addition!

From: _____

_____
(student)

is right on key when it comes to addition!

From: _____